GUERNSEY IN 50 BUILDINGS

SOO WELLFAIR

AMBERLEY

Dedicated to my two wonderful sons and my greatest creations,
Jamie and Thomas

First published 2025

Amberley Publishing, The Hill, Stroud
Gloucestershire GL5 4EP

www.amberley-books.com

British Library Cataloguing in Publication Data.
A catalogue record for this book is available from the British Library.

ISBN 978 1 3981 2038 9 (print)
ISBN 978 1 3981 2039 6 (ebook)

Typesetting by SJmagic DESIGN SERVICES, India.
Printed in Great Britain.

Appointed GPSR EU Representative:
Easy Access System Europe Oü, 16879218
Address: Mustamäe tee 50, 10621, Tallinn, Estonia
Contact Details: gpsr.requests@easproject.com, +358 40 500 3575

Contents

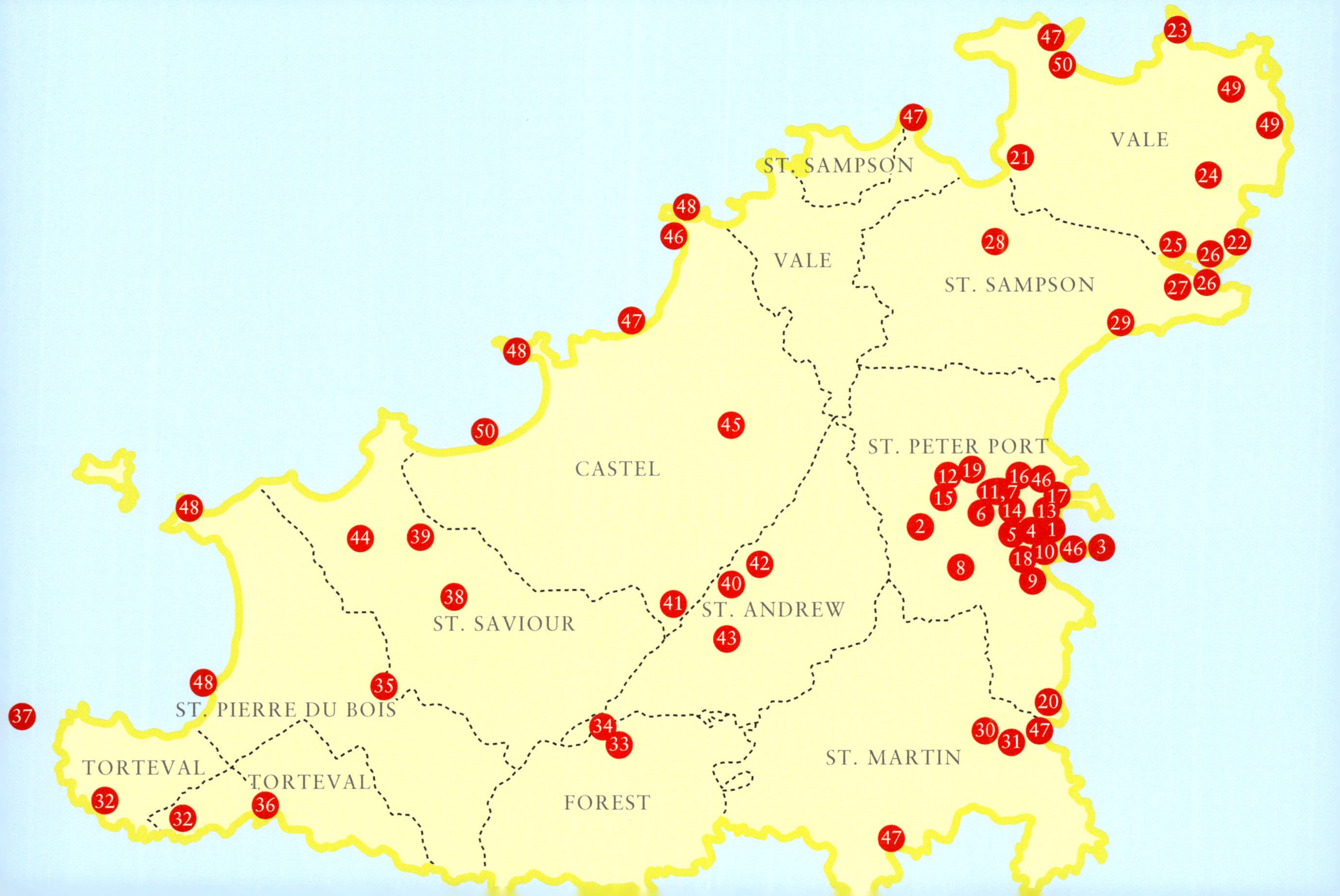
VALE
ST. SAMPSON
VALE
ST. SAMPSON
CASTEL
ST. PETER PORT
ST. ANDREW
ST. SAVIOUR
ST. PIERRE DU BOIS
TORTEVAL
TORTEVAL
FOREST
ST. MARTIN

Key

1. Town Church
2. St Stephen's Church
3. Castle Cornet
4. St Peter Port Market Buildings
5. Guille-Allès Library
6. Elizabeth College
7. Old Government House Hotel
8. Government House
9. Hauteville House
10. No. 26 Cornet Street
11. St James Concert Hall
12. Guernsey Fire Station
13. St Peter Port Constables' Office
14. Royal Court Buildings
15. Victoria Tower
16. Guernsey Police Headquarters
17. States Building, North Plantation
18. Island Archives
19. Priaulx Library
20. Fort George
21. Vale Church
22. Vale Castle
23. Fort Le Marchant
24. Vale Mill
25. Vale Power Station
26. Quarrying Buildings of Northside and Southside
27. St Sampson's Church
28. Oatlands
29. Halfway Tram Stop
30. St Martin's Church
31. Sausmarez Manor
32. Victor Hugo's Haunted House and Mount Herault
33. Forest Church
34. Guernsey Airport
35. St Peter's Church
36. Torteval Church
37. Hanois Lighthouse
38. St Saviour's Church
39. St Saviour's Reservoir
40. St Andrew's Church
41. The Little Chapel
42. Monnaie Chapel
43. German Underground Hospital
44. St Apolline's Chapel
45. Castel Church
46. Repurposed Second World War Bunkers
47. Loophole Towers
48. Guernsey's Three Martello Towers
49. Guernsey Glasshouses
50. Beach Kiosks

Introduction

The Channel Island of Guernsey has a fascinating history, from its earliest prehistoric settlers through to the present day. It was inherited by the English then British Crown as part of the Duchy of Normandy and its individual and separate heritage can be seen throughout the island. This book looks at Guernsey's ten parishes and the most interesting, beautiful and historic buildings in each one. Guernsey's architectural history spans many periods, and the following pages contain examples from the medieval period, Tudor times, the Georgian and Victorian eras, as well as some impressive recent structures. Buildings include the ten parish churches and the church windows created by artist William Morris, the various buildings designed by the celebrated architect John Wilson, buildings constructed using the locally quarried granite, castles, forts, towers and an extremely atmospheric underground Second World War hospital. Our journey of Guernsey's most fascinating buildings begins with the parish church in the harbour town of St Peter Port.

The 50 Buildings

1. Town Church

The island of Guernsey is divided into ten parishes, with each parish having its own parish church. In the beautiful harbour town of St Peter Port, overlooking the seafront is the parish church of St Peter Port. Officially named the Town Church of St Peter, Apostle and Martyr, it is more commonly known as simply

St Peter Port's Town Church. (Soo Wellfair)

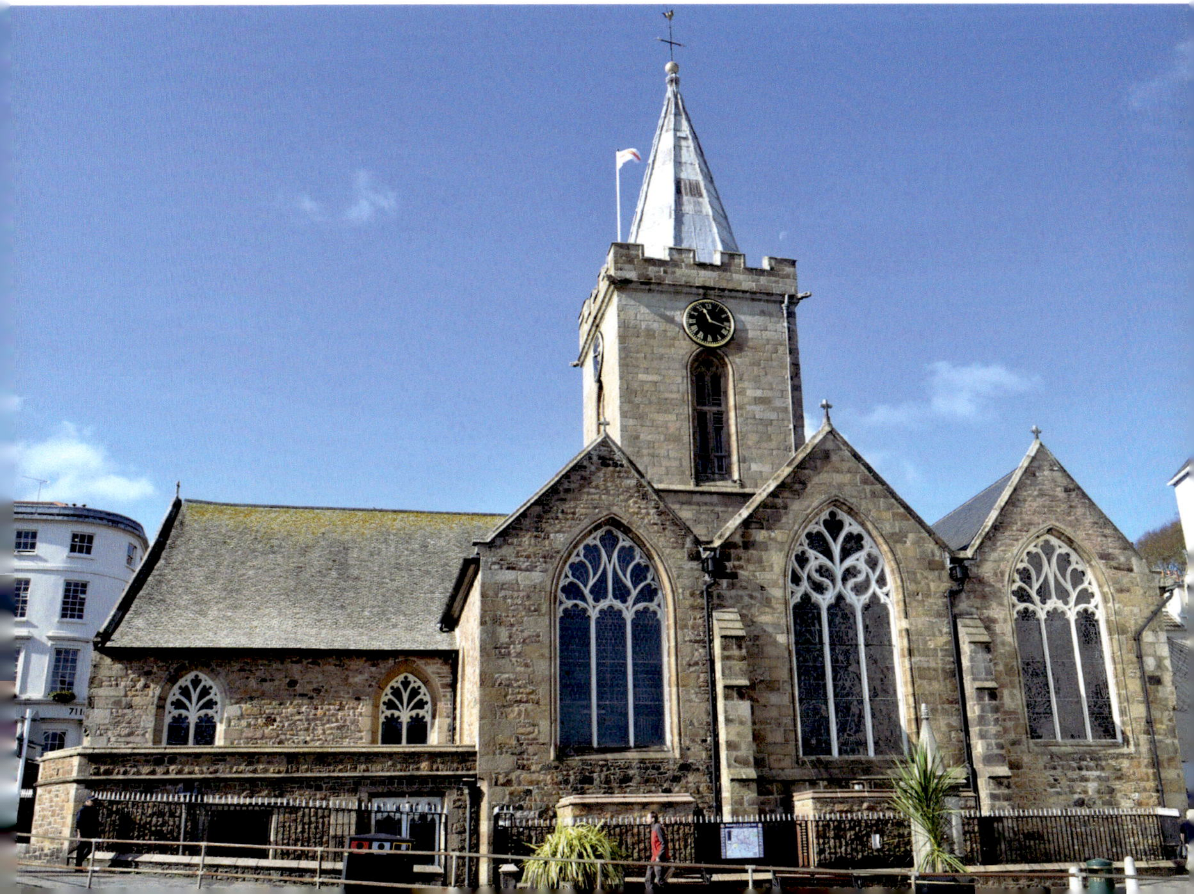

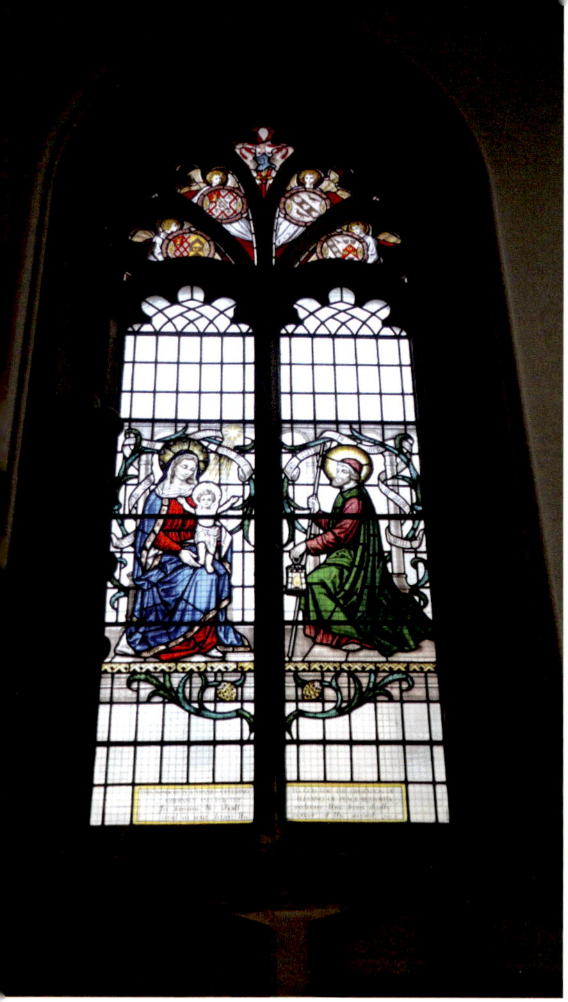

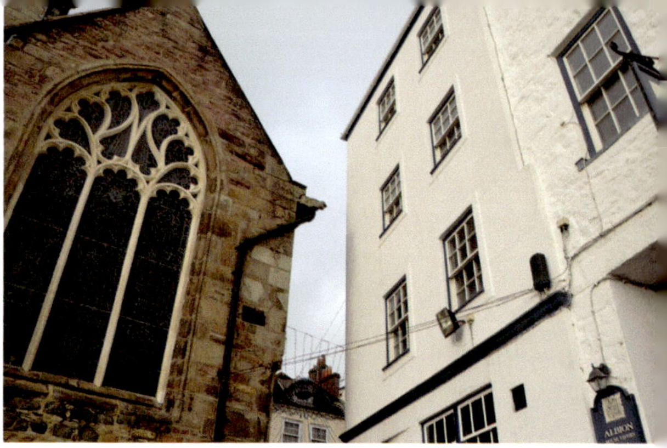

Above: The church gargoyle. (Soo Wellfair)

Left: The Liberation Window. (Soo Wellfair)

Below: German road marking. (Soo Wellfair)

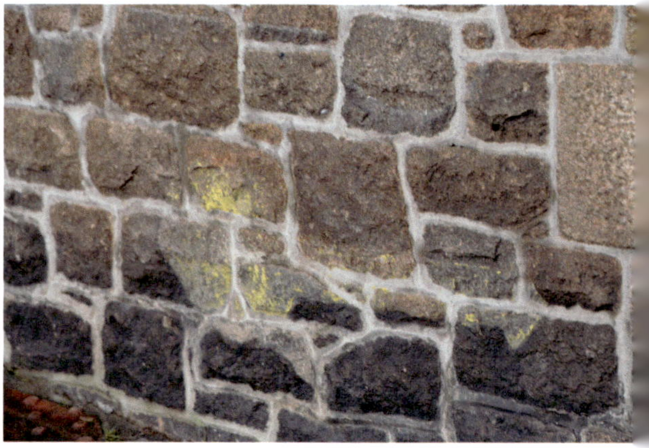

the Town Church. Like many churches, it is likely that it was built on the site of a former holy building. Early records reference a church being built by order of William the Conqueror on the same site, back in the eleventh century. The oldest part of the church is the Norman archway, which forms part of the nave of the church. There are also thicker parts of the church walls which may have been parts of the original building, incorporated into a fourteenth- or fifteenth-century rebuild. There have been countless changes to the church over the years, with the current spire being added in the eighteenth century and a significant restoration project, headed up by well-known architect John Wilson, taking place in the nineteenth century. The Town Church was once surrounded by a variety of buildings and dwellings which were demolished over time, yet one building remains in very close proximity to the church. The Albion Tavern next door is believed by many to be the pub closest to a church in the British Isles, all thanks to the gargoyle which protrudes from the church towards the pub.

The window over the high altar is named the Liberation Window. It was installed as a way to commemorate Guernsey's Liberation Day, which takes place on 9 May every year. The church has nine bells, named Liberty, Promise,

Hope, Freedom, Saviour, Vega, Michael, Peter and Trinity. They are known collectively as the Liberation Bells.

During the occupation years (1940–45) the occupying forces introduced a new road naming system based on numbers and colours. These new routes were often marked on the sides of buildings. Many have faded over time and others restored. Those with good eyesight may be able to spot one of these road markings on the outside of the Town Church. The best place to view it is across the road from the church at 'Loafer's Wall', at the bottom of Fountain Street.

2. St Stephen's Church

St Stephen's Church can be considered St Peter Port's second parish church, and is the youngest parish church in Guernsey. As St Peter Port expanded over the years and the population expanded rapidly, the Town Church was no longer able to accommodate all those living in the parish. St Stephen's Church was to become the town's second Anglican church. The foundation stone was laid in 1862 and the church was fully consecrated and operational by 1866. The church was designed by the English Gothic Revival architect George Fredrick Bodley. The style is reminiscent of buildings from the thirteenth century with its long, narrow windows and beautiful, tall arches. It was constructed using a combination of Caen stone, as well as locally quarried pink and blue granite. In the 1850s Bodley had struck up a friendship and working partnership with the celebrated designer

St Stephen's Church. (Soo Wellfair)

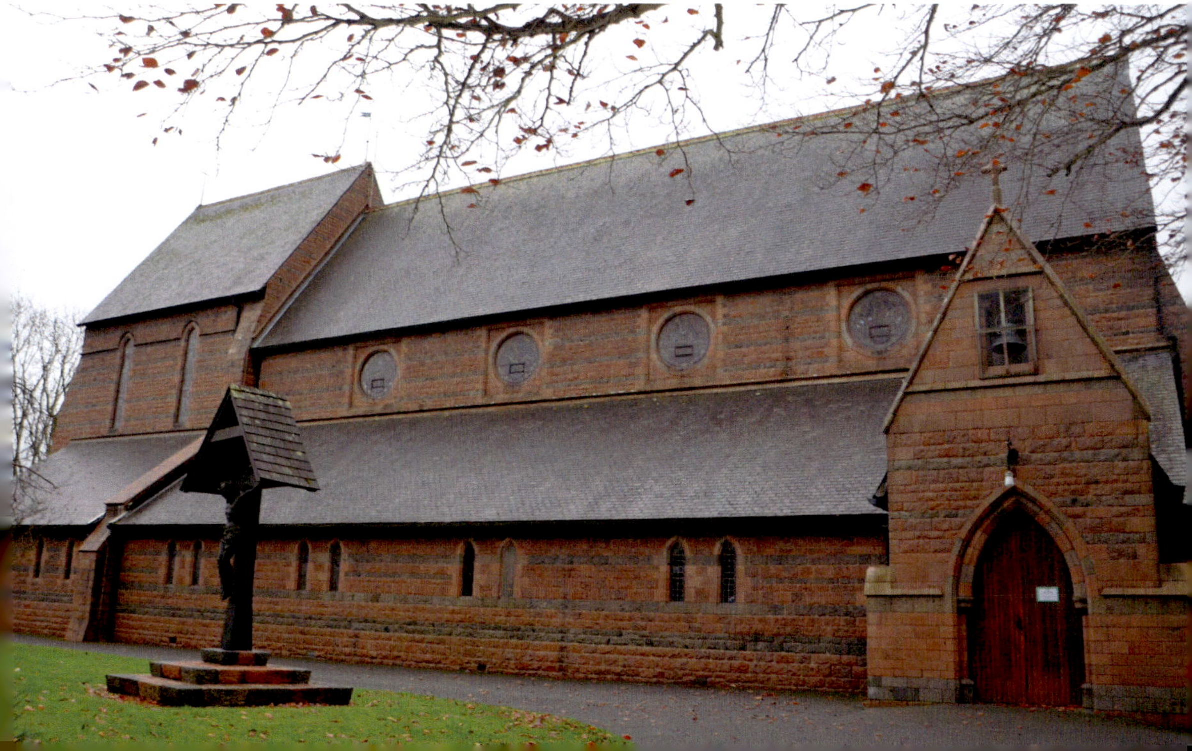

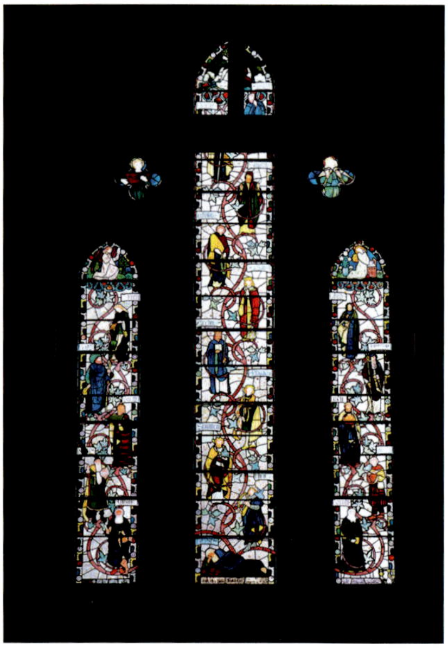

Tree of Jesse window by William Morris. (Soo Wellfair)

William Morris. It should come as no surprise then, that some of St Stephen's stained-glass windows are designed by Morris and his team. The most impressive of these William Morris windows is the Tree of Jesse window, which depicts the lineage of Jesus Christ. With so many beautiful, large windows, it is no surprise that St Stephen's is one of the most stunning churches on the island. At times it is absolutely flooded with light and colour.

In 1892 the Chapel of the Incarnation was added to the church. In fact, it had been salvaged from a nearby church, which was being demolished to make room for the development of the Royal Court buildings.

3. Castle Cornet

Castle Cornet, in its original form, was built in the early thirteenth century as a response to the threat of French invasion after Guernsey became loyal to the English Crown. It was initially quite a small castle, perched on an island and cut off completely from the land at high tide. It was designed in such a way that it could only be attacked by sea, which was much more difficult. Over the years the castle has been expanded and modified, with extensive expansion taking place in the medieval and Tudor times, large-scale reinforcements in the Victorian era and some significant additions during the Second World War. The buildings within the castle walls, therefore, are quite diverse.

The clock tower is an attractive feature of the castle, with the workings of the clock on display within the tower. Originally, the tower was used as Guernsey's main prison and would have been used to hold those awaiting trial. One of

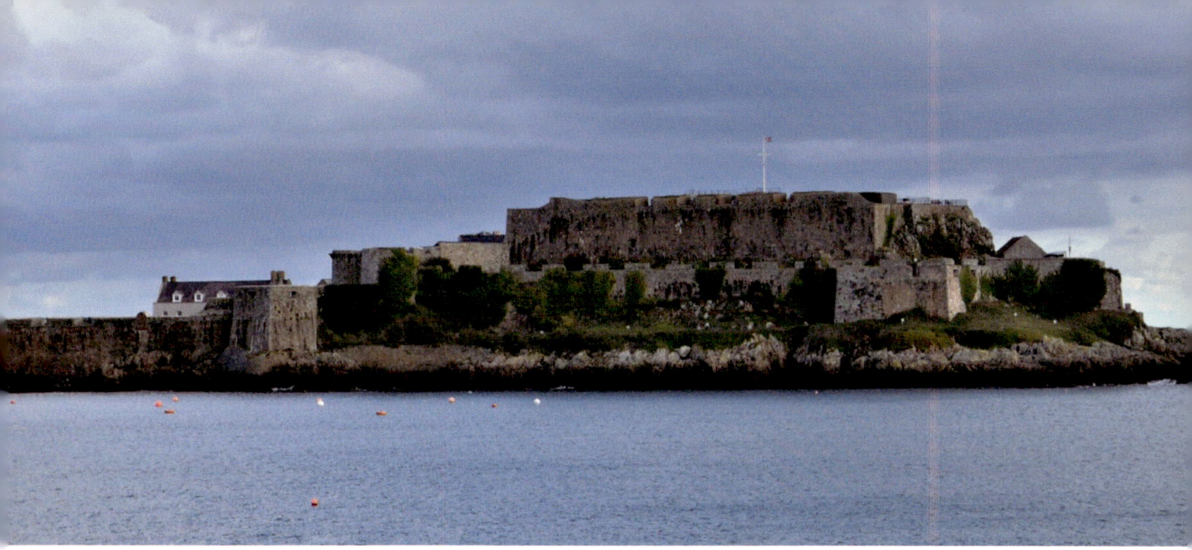

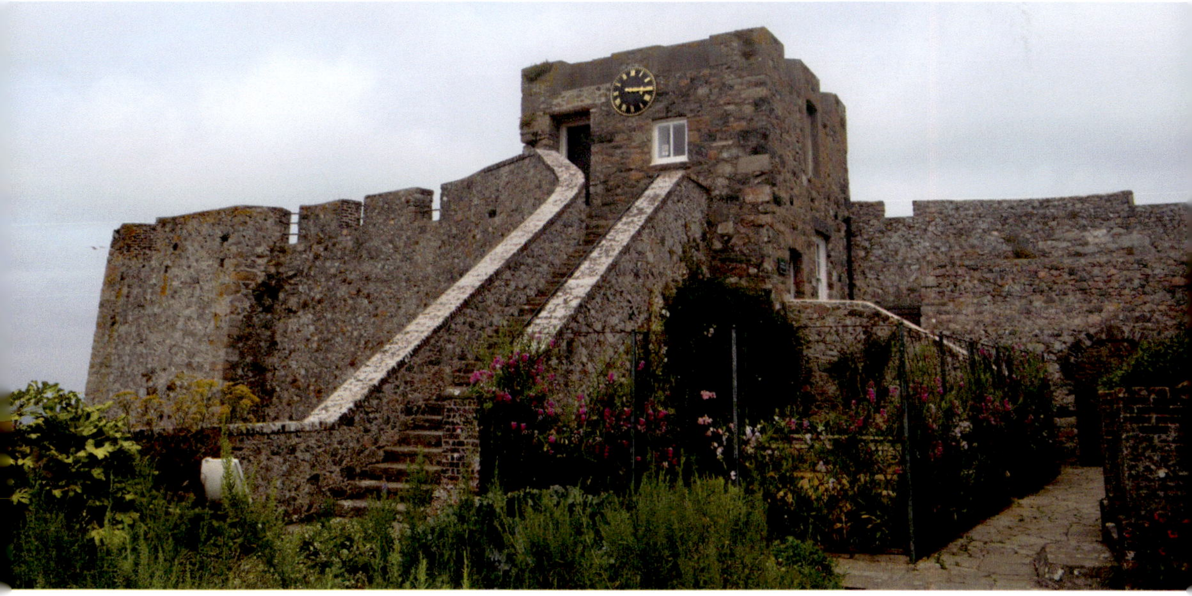

Top: Castle Cornet. (Soo Wellfair)

Above: Clock tower and former prison. (Soo Wellfair)

Right: General Lambert's garden. (Soo Wellfair)

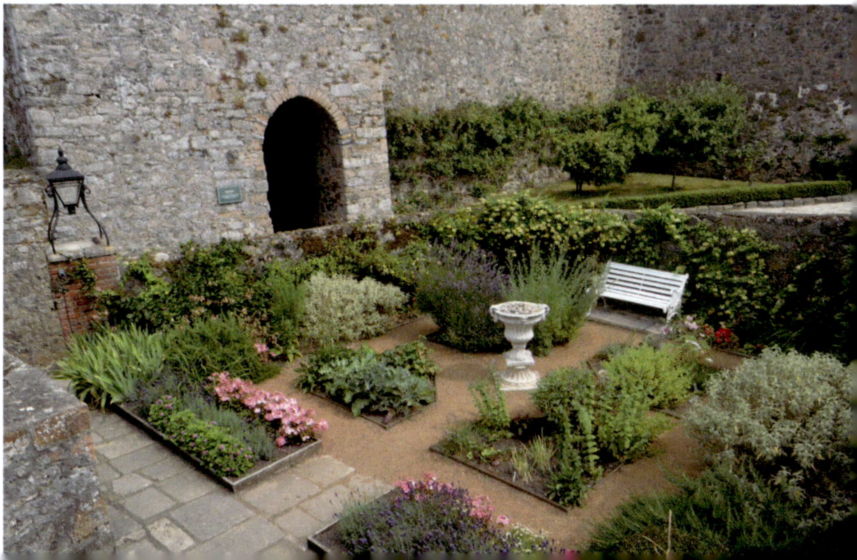

the castle's most famous inmates was General John Lambert, a high-ranking Parliamentarian who escaped execution after the English Civil War. Granted his own garden to tend during his incarceration, General Lambert's garden remains a popular feature of the castle today.

The castle was heavily fortified during the occupation years, with a large number of bunkers and gun placements added to the existing structure. Made predominantly from reinforced concrete, these modern additions are notably conspicuous and quite a contrast to their surroundings.

4. St Peter Port Market Buildings

Historically, the market has moved around Guernsey to move with the needs of the ever-growing population and the expansion of the harbour. Originally based in the centre of the island, the market gradually moved to its current position in St Peter Port, where it was more conveniently located for the port and sea trade. There would have once been dedicated areas for meat, fish, fruit, vegetables and flowers and it was a busy, thriving public market until the late twentieth century, when the buildings gradually became retail spaces.

One of the most iconic buildings within the market area is the former meat market, which dates back to 1822. This is another example of the work of

St Peter Port Market. (Soo Wellfair)

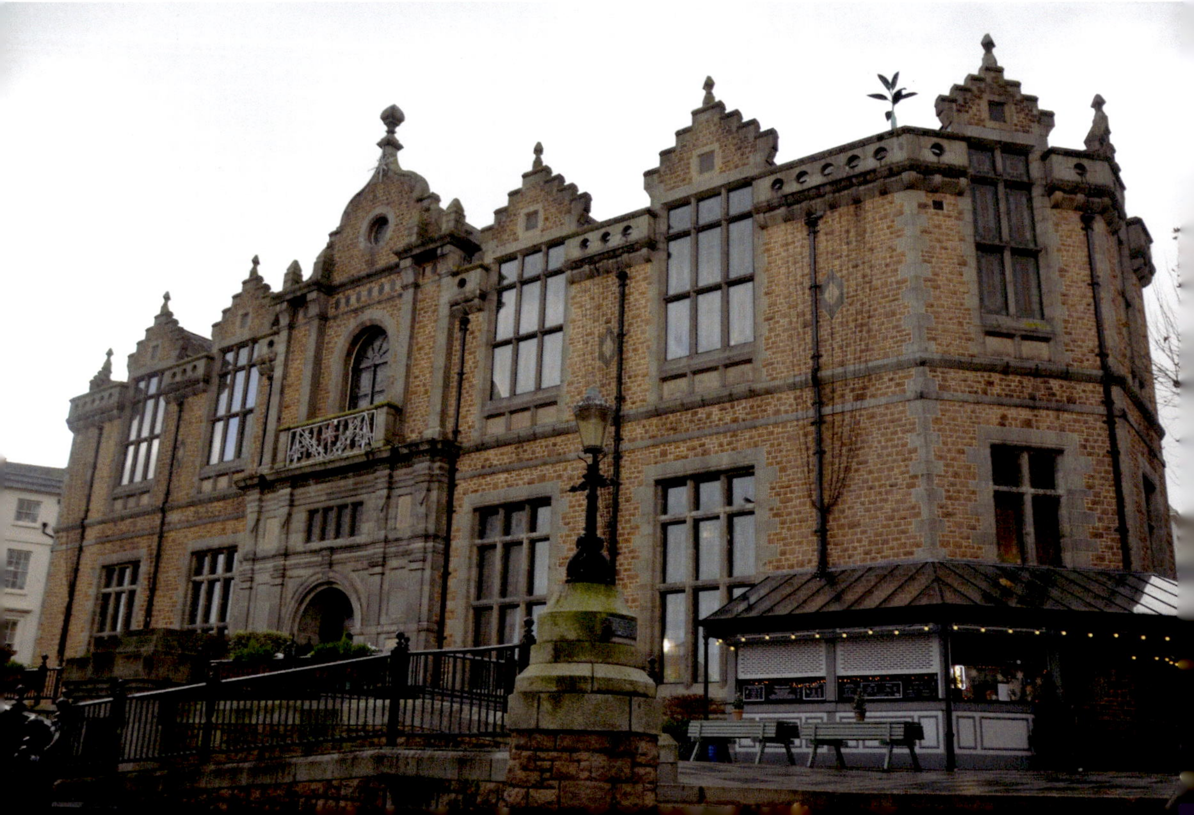

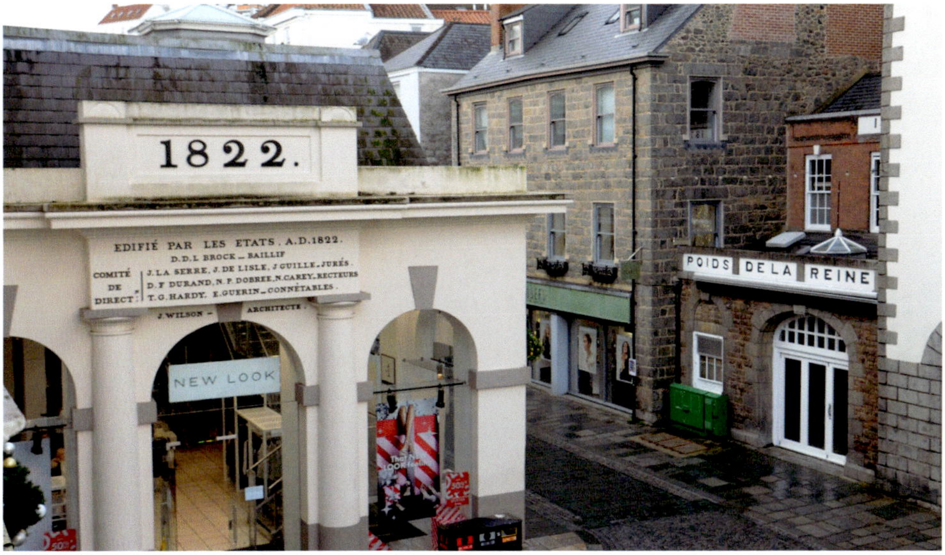

The old meat market and Poids de la Reine. (Soo Wellfair)

architect John Wilson, and it was very much designed with practicality in mind. Whilst being a beautiful building in its own right with features reminiscent of Greek architecture, the focus of the interior was to provide maximum space for the various butchers' stalls and with easy access for their customers. One design technique used to maximise selling space was to make the hall entirely without windows, leaving every inch of wall space to be utilised by stalls and displays. The Inner Street linked the meat and fish markets with the lower vegetable market, which also had fruit and flowers on offer.

Across the other side of the market square you would have found the French Halles (now a retail shop) and next to it the former Poids de la Reine. Built in 1876, the Queen's Weights building was used after an official weights and measures system was introduced to the market. The signage is still there today, featuring prominently in the modern market area.

The market area is still a busy and thriving part of St Peter Port. Regular 'pop-up' markets are held in the market square, as well as many popular community events throughout the year such as family fun days, live music and performances, art events and exhibitions and the yearly switching on of the Christmas lights.

5. Guille-Allès Library

The Guille-Allès public library in the heart of St Peter Port is one of Guernsey's most valuable and well-used resources. Built in 1782, it was designed and used as a place of recreation for high society. Known as the Assembly Halls, it was a venue for socialising, dancing and networking. It was an extremely fashionable

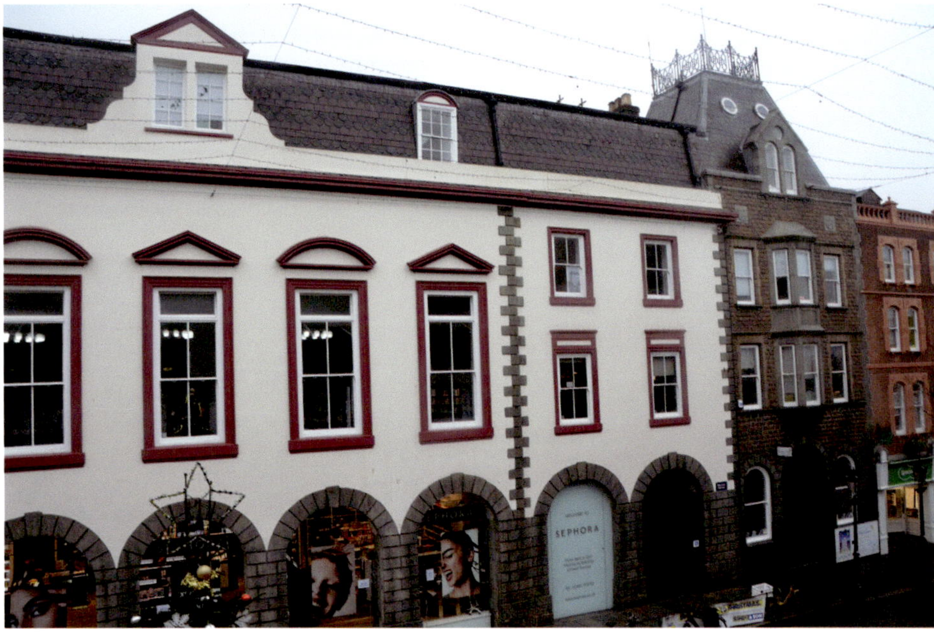

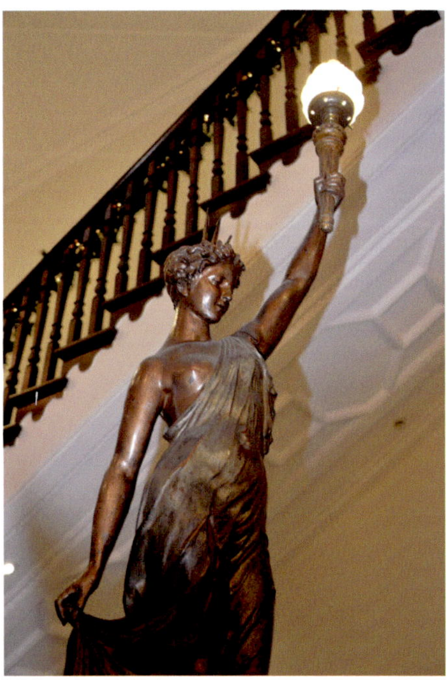

Above: Guille-Allès Library. (Soo Wellfair)

Left: Bronze statue on staircase. (Soo Wellfair)

Below: Guille-Allès stained-glass window. (Soo Wellfair)

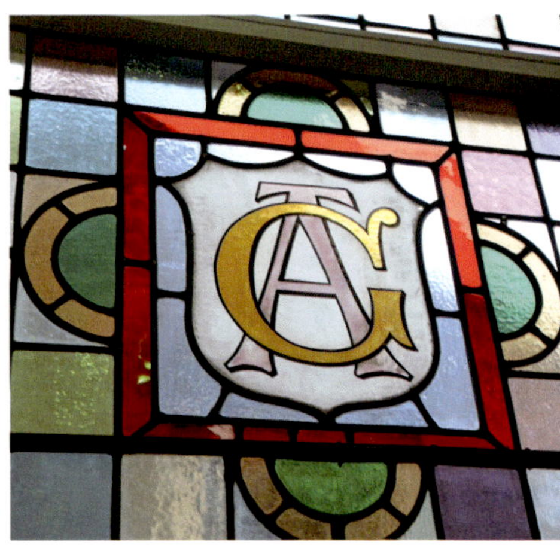

and exclusive part of Georgian life with around thirty assembly evenings held per year. In 1882 it was to become the Guille-Allès Library, named after its founders Thomas Guille and Frederick Allès. These two childhood friends came up with their idea for the library whilst both working as apprentices in Manhattan in the

1830s. It was Guille that was first inspired after seeing a magnificent library in the city and when he and his good friend returned to their homeland of Guernsey, they made their vision a reality by leasing the former Assembly Rooms. A further extension, which was built in 1888, created what we now know as the grand library entrance and staircase. One of the most striking features of the hallway is the original 1888 tiled flooring, which cost the library the tidy sum of £68. Thousands of tiles in sage green, white, buff and chocolate were used to create the beautiful pattern, which greets visitors to the library and still looks most impressive today. The two beautiful bronze torch-bearing figures that can be found at the foot of the great staircase are certainly inspired by the magnificent Manhattan library that first captivated the library's founders.

An interesting architectural feature of the library is the Widow's Walk, which makes up the tower at the very top of the 1888 building. The ornate iron railing and circular tower windows were typical of towers built in North American coastal homes back when Guille and Allès were resident there. The Widow's Walk has a rather sad back story, with these structures being added to homes so the wives of mariners might look out for their husbands whilst away at sea, often never to return.

6. Elizabeth College

Visitors to Guernsey often enquire about the 'big castle' that can be spotted high up on the St Peter Port skyline. Despite its impressive towers and crenellated appearance, the building in question is actually an independent co-educational school named Elizabeth College. The college was originally established in 1563 by order of Queen Elizabeth I and was intended as a place of education for boys planning on entering the church. The original school did not flourish, struggling over the years to find both staff and students and was given a new lease of life in the early nineteenth century when it was re-chartered then rebuilt by the famed architect John Wilson. The foundation stone was laid in 1826 and completed in 1829. Since then, the school has become a well-respected and successful place of education, with former pupils known as 'Old Elizabethans'. Elizabeth College has educated many well-known individuals over the years, including the writer P. G. Wodehouse.

It is an impressive building and possibly one of Wilson's finest projects during his tenure in Guernsey. It is quite symmetrical in design, with square towers and a taller central tower with four octagonal pinnacles in each corner. It is this tower that is visible from the harbour and is often mistaken for a fortress, although this part of the design has often been criticised for being a little out of scale with the rest of the building and thought to be a little on the squat side. That aside, it is still a striking and iconic building. The old porter's lodge gateway is still an attractive and quirky feature, although no longer used as an entrance to the college.

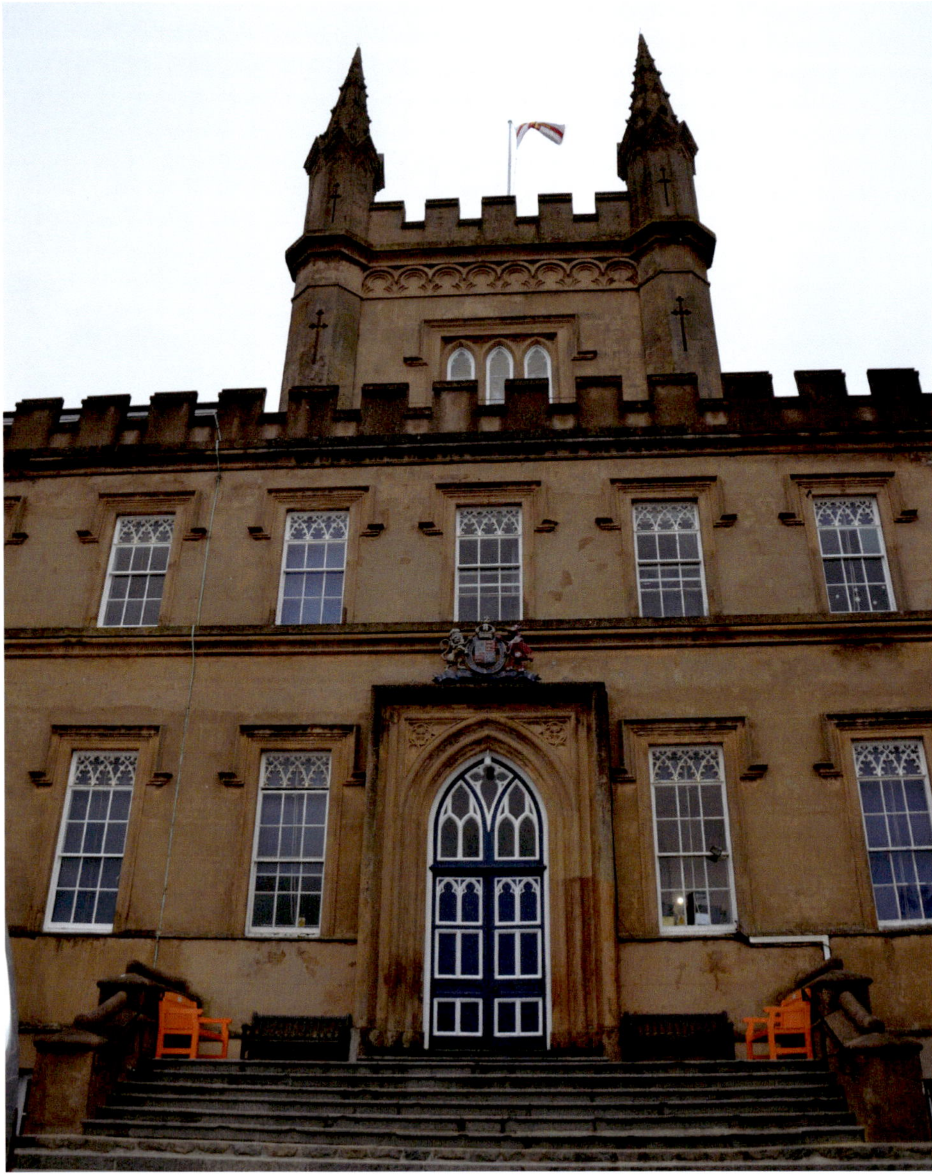

Elizabeth College. (Soo Wellfair)

The main college building has some hidden gems in terms of features. One example can be found near the top of the building; an area now set aside for storage. This is where the former detention cells are located. What makes these tiny rooms so interesting (besides the obligatory ghost stories) are the carvings on the walls. Each student of the college is assigned a unique identity number and back when the cells were used to punish unruly pupils, it became quite the tradition to carve names and numbers into the cell walls.

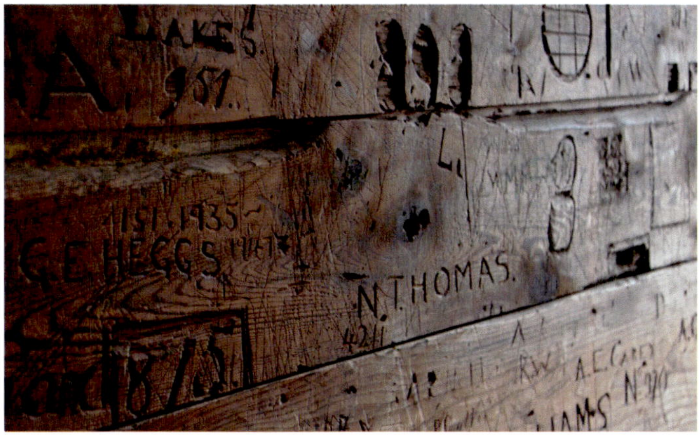

Detention cell engravings. (Soo Wellfair)

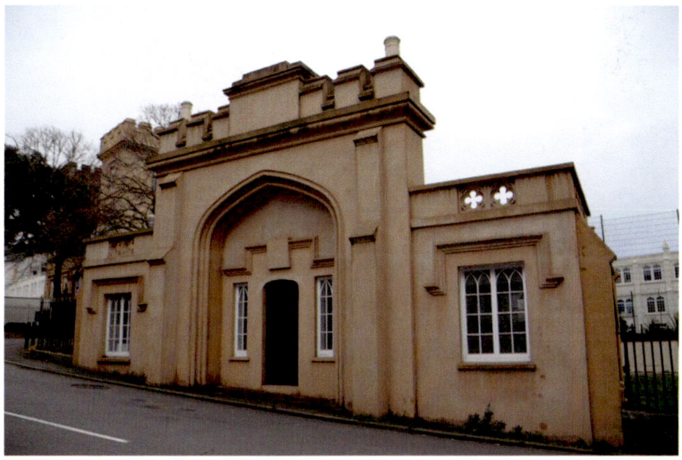

Old porter's lodge. (Soo Wellfair)

7. Old Government House Hotel

Now known as Guernsey's only five-star hotel and referred to simply as the 'OGH', the Old Government House Hotel in St Peter Port has quite an illustrious history. It was built in the early seventeenth century as the residence of a wealthy merchant and by the end of that century had been purchased by the States of Guernsey for the island's Lieutenant-Governor, which is how it got its current name. It remained the official residence of the Lieutenant-Governor until 1857 when it was opened as a hotel for the first time.

During the occupation years, many of Guernsey's largest houses and hotels were requisitioned by the occupying forces. Some were set up as official army headquarters and offices, whilst others were used to house German soldiers. The OGH was primarily used as a *soldatenheim*, which translates quite simply as 'soldiers' home'. This was a place where German soldiers could relax when off duty. Some fabulous old photos from these days are on display in the hotel.

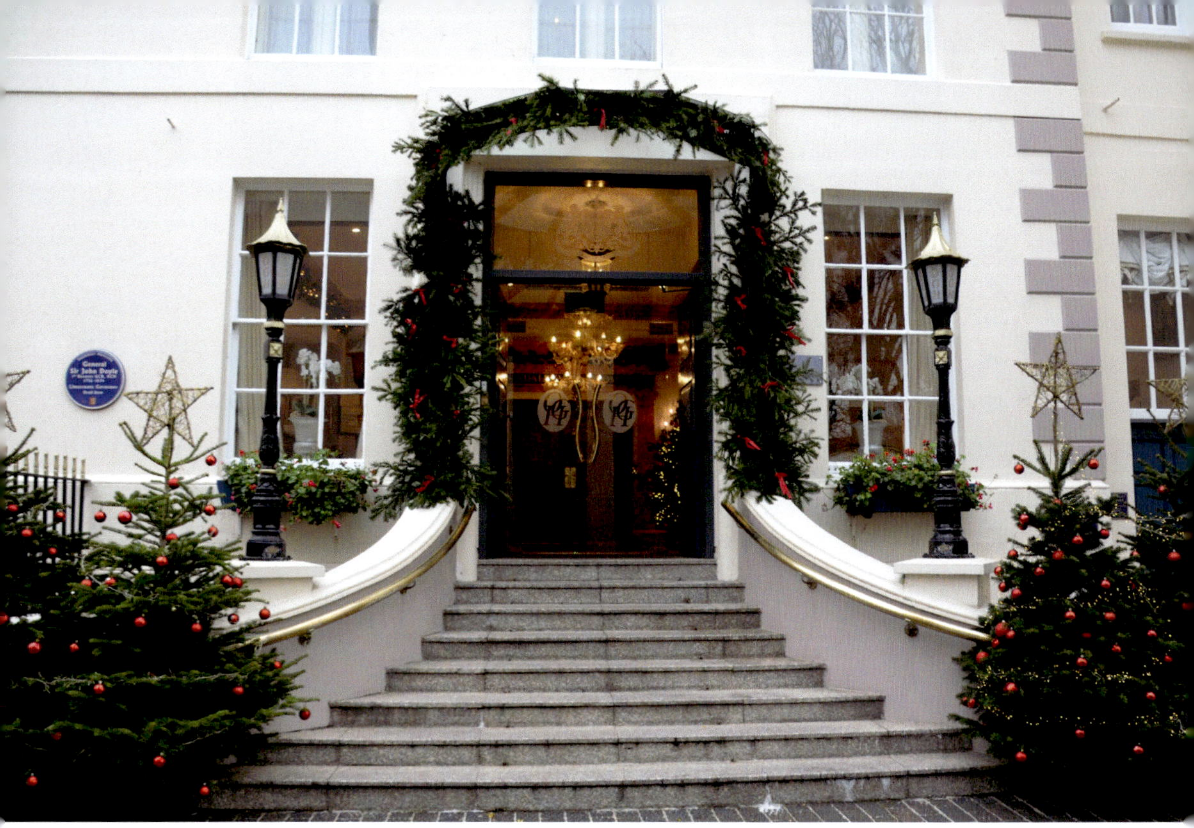

Above: Old Government House Hotel. (Soo Wellfair)

Below: Original front entrance in restaurant. (Soo Wellfair)

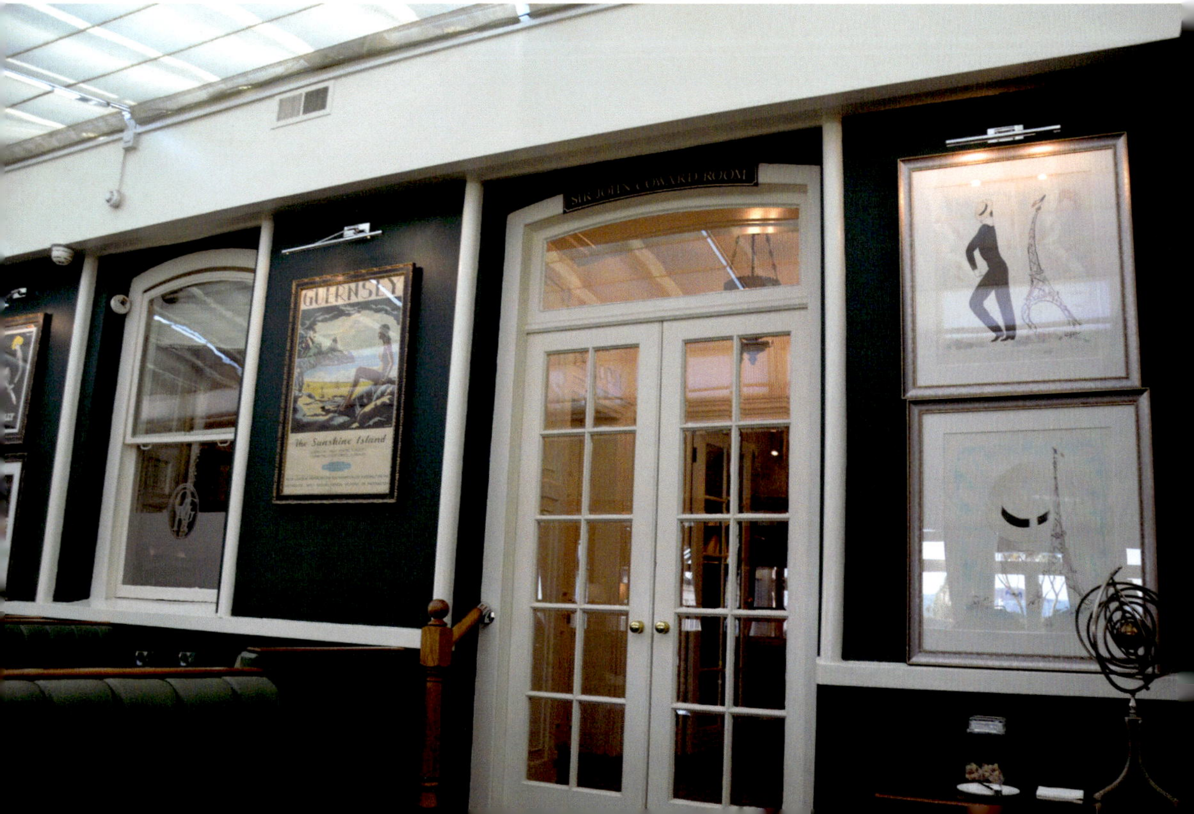

The eighteenth-century Crown Office, which was created back when the building was in governmental use, is still very much part of the hotel. Naturally the building has changed, with various additions and extensions over the years. However, eagle-eyed diners in the main restaurant may notice a very clear reminder of the original house and its footprint. The wall and doorway, which essentially divides the restaurant area from the main hotel, is in fact the original outer entrance of the building.

8. Government House

Government House, a beautiful Georgian home found on the outskirts of St Peter Port, is the home and office of Guernsey's Lieutenant-Governor. The Lieutenant-Governor is the sovereign's personal representative of the Crown throughout the Bailiwick of Guernsey. The role of Lieutenant-Governor is similar to that of a head of state and includes responsibilities such as acting on behalf of the sovereign during ceremonial occasions, granting royal assent to new legislation, attending governmental meetings and liaising with the UK government. The Lieutenant-Governor also acts as the officer in charge of the British Armed Forces within the Bailiwick jurisdiction. The house is not open to the public as it is a private home and office. However, Government House is used to host charitable events, royal and ambassadorial visits and ceremonial events throughout the year.

This beautiful property was built as a private residence in the 1780s and originally named Le Mont, which later became The Mount. It's had several redesigns and refurbishments since it was built, notably the decision to completely flip the layout of the house in 1869. The house initially faced away from the main road, but over time the front and rear outlooks of the house were reversed. Soon after, the long driveway leading up to what is now the front aspect of the house was added. It became Government House as we know it in the late 1940s, when

Government House front aspect. (Soo Wellfair)

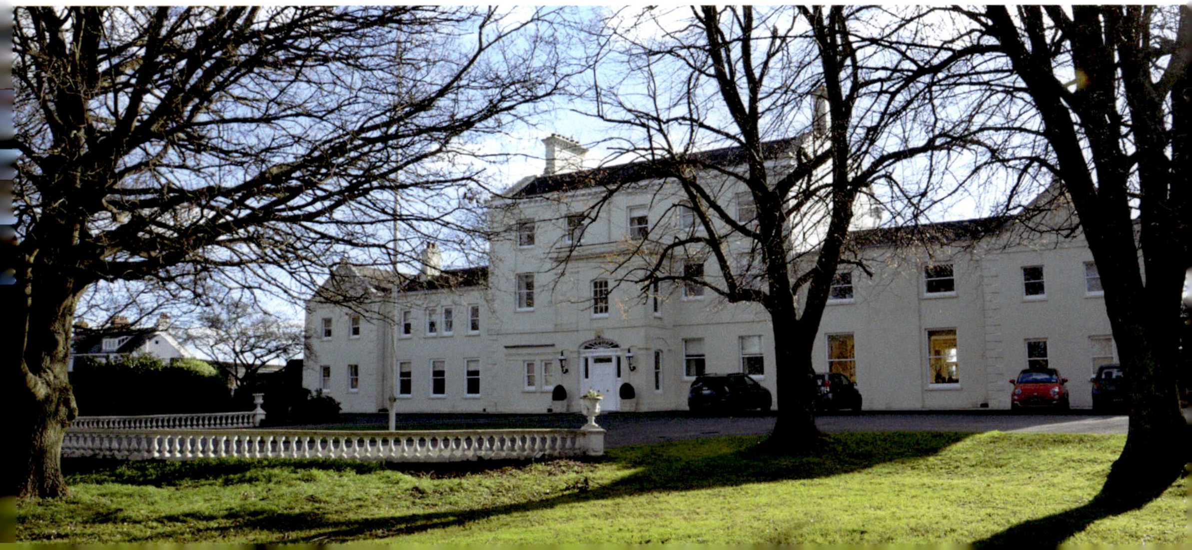

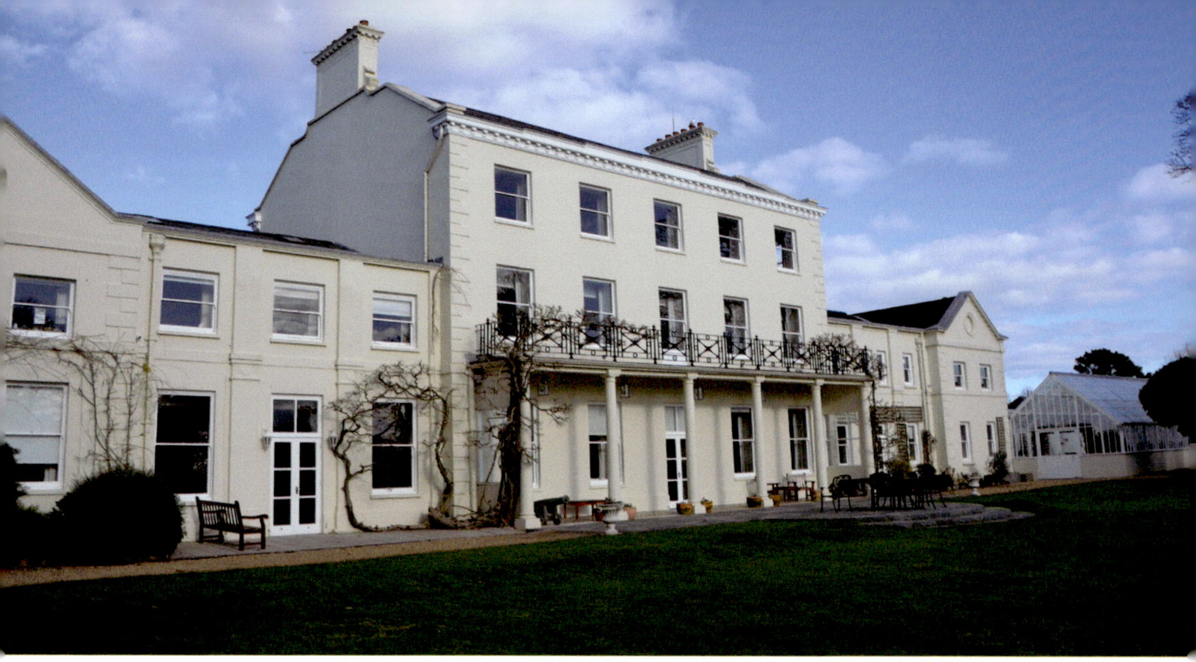

Above: Government House rear aspect. (Soo Wellfair)

Below: Government House reception room. (Soo Wellfair)

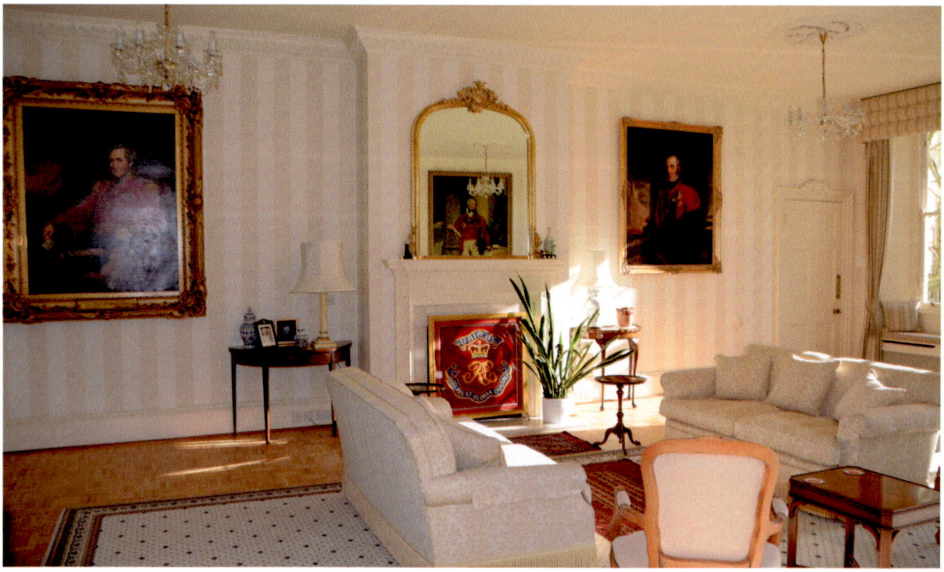

it was gifted to Guernsey by the Crown as a permanent residence for all future Lieutenant-Governors.

Government House is set within beautiful grounds covering around 10 acres of land with around 150 mature trees. It also has its very own Victorian walled garden, which is still used to grow fruit, vegetables and flowers for the house. It also has a lovely rear patio which was created using repurposed flagstones removed from the Guernsey Fire Station when their vehicle bays were modernised.

9. Hauteville House

This beautiful townhouse, built around the turn of the nineteenth century for a wealthy privateer, sits proudly in the elevated area of Hauteville, overlooking the sea and St Peter Port. Its most well-known owner was the French writer Victor Hugo, who lived in Guernsey between 1855 and 1870. During this time, he worked on many of his novels and plays. Hugo spent fourteen years in Hauteville House and lavishly decorated it in his own eccentric style. The house is built on five floors and is considered to be a work of art from top to bottom. It was Hugo's belief that a house should be considered a blank canvas and every square inch of the interior should be decorated. He worked closely with local craftsmen to build and customise a lot of the furniture in the house. Many of the larger items of furniture inside have been carved with quotes or scenes that reflected Hugo's beliefs and ideologies. There are also many items that could be considered quite 'quirky'. A good example would be the Ancestors' Chair. This grand, decorative dining chair was reserved for the spirits of Hugo's departed ancestors should any wish to visit during mealtimes.

The house was donated to the city of Paris in 1927 and is open to the public as a museum, with guided tours running throughout the summer season. You can also visit the beautiful gardens and the 'Oak of the United States of Europe', which

Below left: Hauteville House rear aspect and gardens. (Soo Wellfair)

Below right: Inside Hauteville House. (Soo Wellfair)

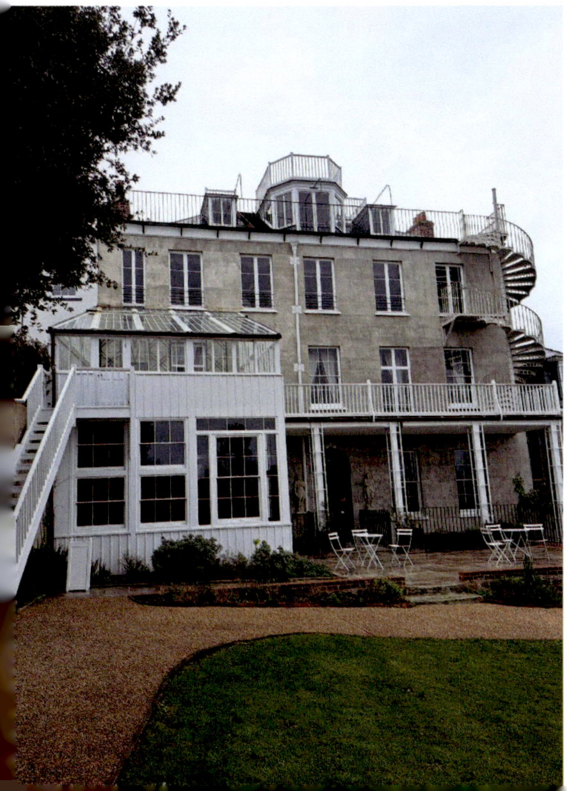

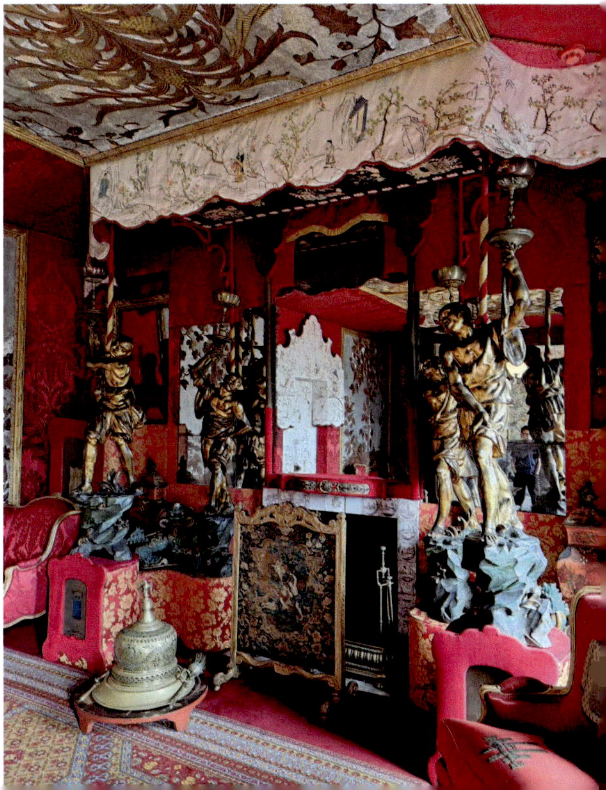

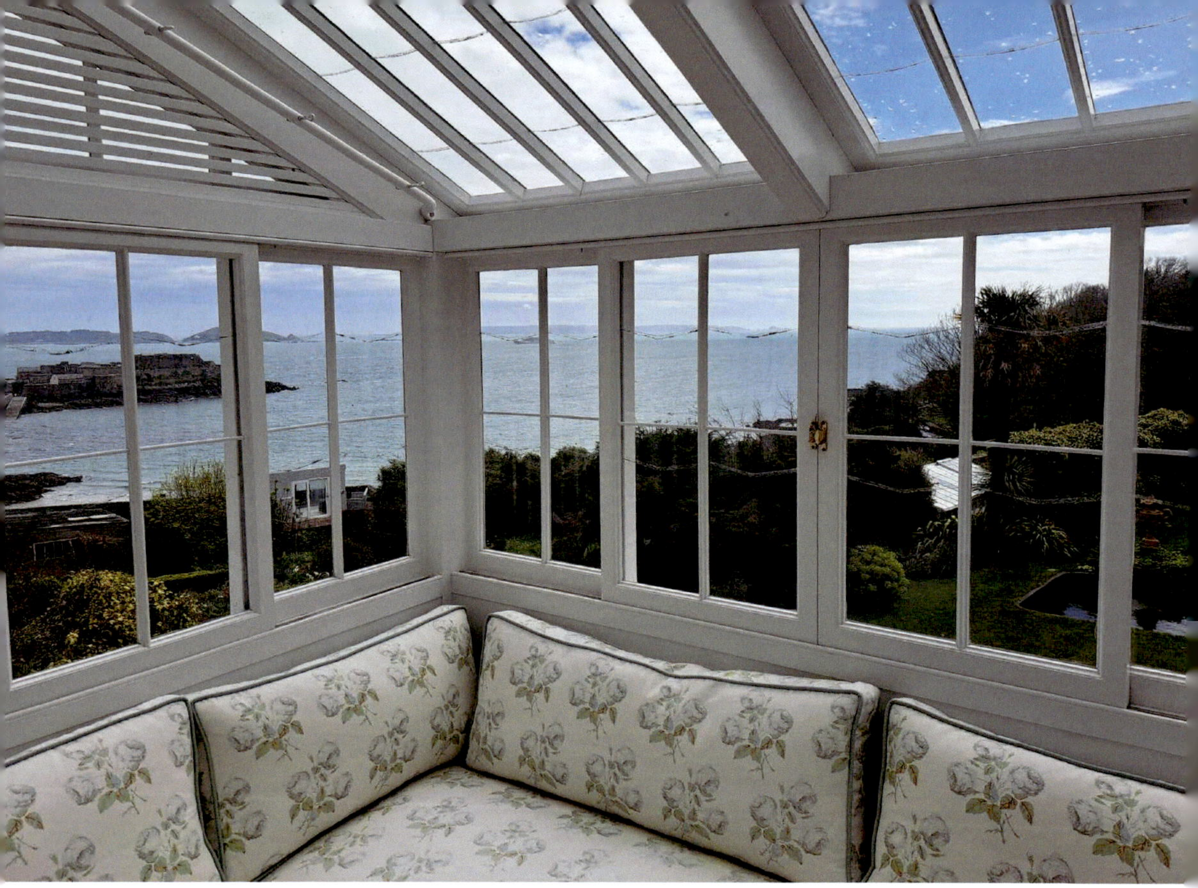

The view from Victor Hugo's conservatory. (Soo Wellfair)

started out as an acorn planted by Hugo and his grandchildren. In 2018 a wealthy businessman donated £2.6 million, which enabled an extensive restoration of the property to take place.

10. No. 26 Cornet Street

The Victorian shop and parlour really is a hidden gem of Guernsey. No. 26 Cornet Street is thought to be one of the oldest standing buildings in St Peter Port, with the original structure dating back to medieval times. This is quite a rarity as although we know there was a medieval town, very little remains from those early days of Guernsey's little harbour town. Although much of what we can see today of the building dates back to the eighteenth century with some nineteenth-century modifications, it is still an important historical site. One of the building's most interesting features is a striking set of double bow windows, complete with bespoke curved shutters which are still operated using the original mechanical turn-handle. During Victorian times No. 26 Cornet Street was a confectionery shop with living quarters for the shopkeeper's family. Today, this setup has been lovingly recreated for the modern visitor. Open to the public and run by the

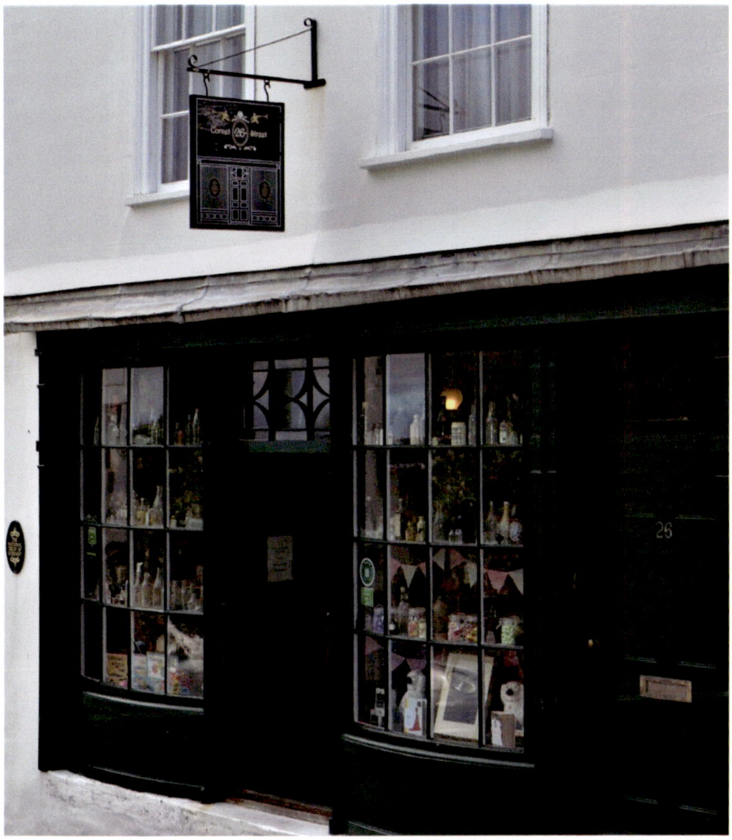

Right: No. 26 Cornet Street. (Soo Wellfair)

Below: Inside No. 26 Cornet Street. (Soo Wellfair)

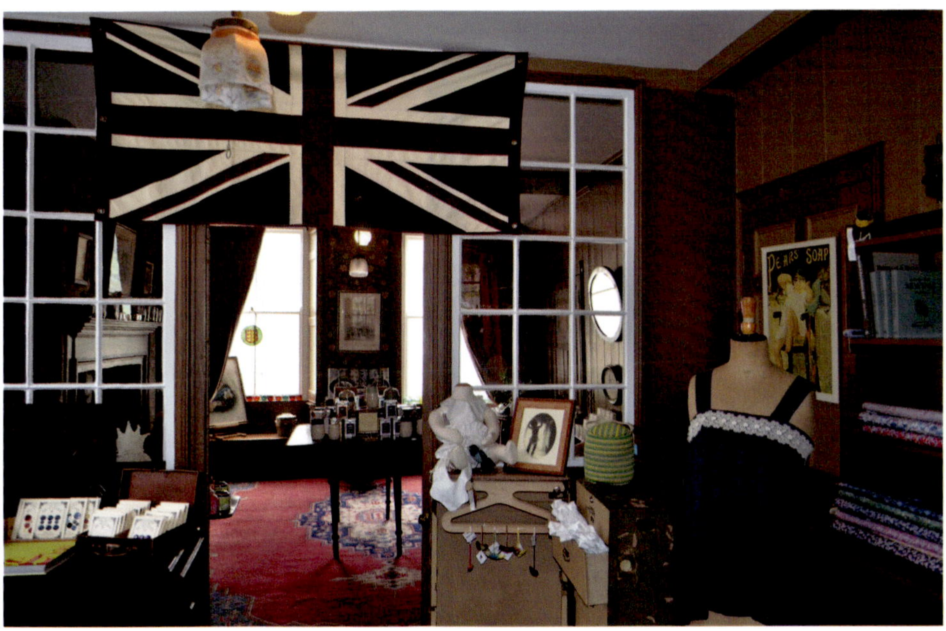

National Trust of Guernsey, No. 26 Cornet Street can be considered part shop, part museum and offers a fascinating snapshot of Victorian life. In the shop you can treat yourself to some of your favourite childhood sweets, which are sold by weight (metric and imperial). You will also find a delightful selection of gifts and crafts to purchase, many handmade locally and in the UK and ethically sourced. In the beautifully restored parlour you will find an eclectic display of Victoriana.

11. St James Concert Hall

St James is another of Guernsey's iconic buildings that make up the impressive St Peter Port Harbour skyline, with its iconic domed tower dominating this view of town. It was originally named St James the Less, built in 1818 as a church for the members of the British army, regularly garrisoned in Guernsey. As church services in Guernsey were still largely given in French at this time, it was felt that an alternative was needed for the ever-expanding military community and any other English speaking islanders. It was designed by the popular architect

Below left: St James Concert Hall. (Soo Wellfair)

Below right: St James stage area. (Soo Wellfair)

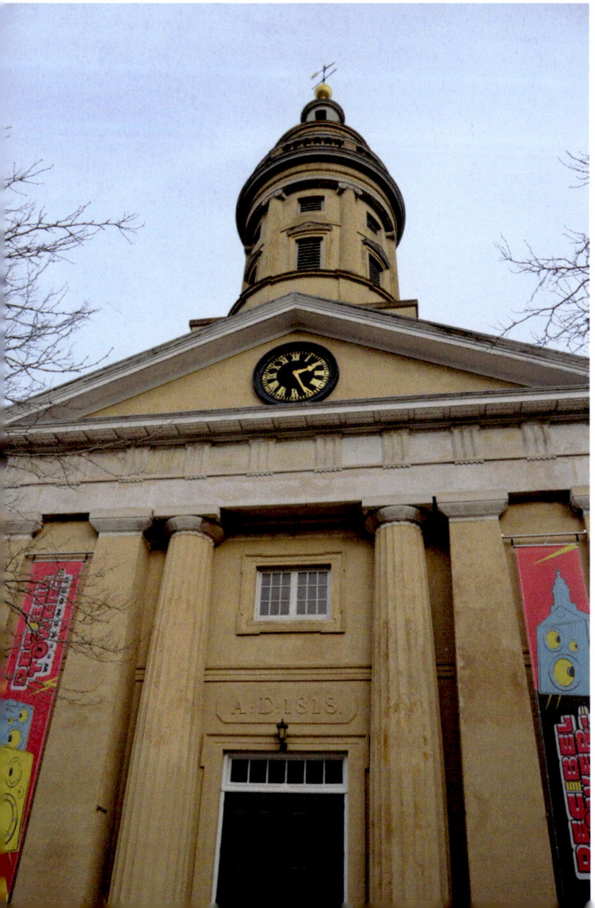

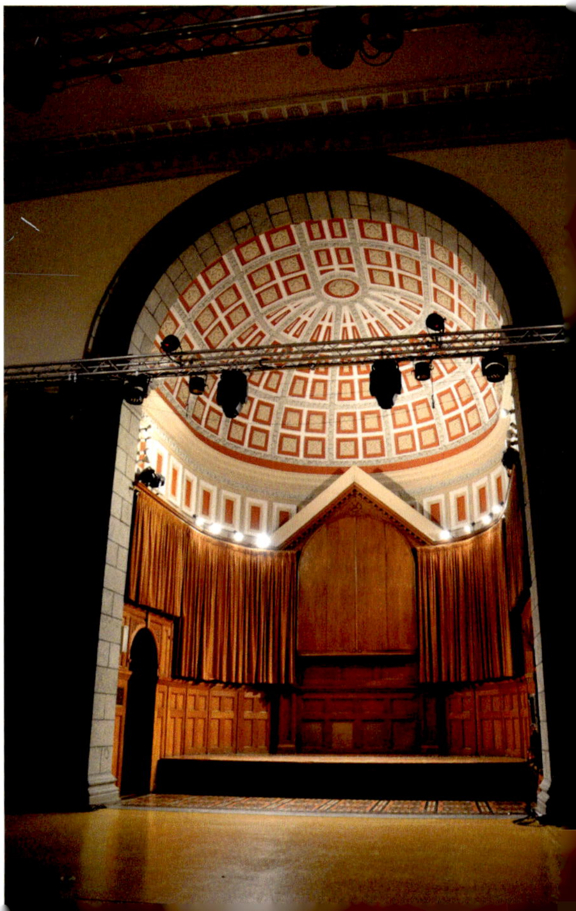

John Wilson, although the basic plans are attributed to an unknown designer known only as Mr Brookes.

Although it was very well used during its time as a church, by the 1970s St James had fallen into disrepair and was under threat of demolition. Fortunately, thanks to local resistance, plus a vast amount of fundraising and campaigning, St James was saved and reborn as a concert and assembly hall in 1985.

St James now hosts a large number of entertainment events throughout the year including classical and modern concerts, theatrical productions, comedy nights, community events, literary talks and much more. It is also an extremely popular wedding venue as it remains a beautiful piece of architecture and is visually impressive, both inside and out.

12. Guernsey Fire Station

The Guernsey Fire and Rescue Service has its headquarters in a beautiful mid-nineteenth century grey granite listed building, opposite the Victoria Tower. The building was built in 1850 for the Royal Guernsey Militia. It would have been used as the island's main base for the Militia and was known as the Town Arsenal. It would have served several purposes as the Militia headquarters, including being used as a drill hall to facilitate training. In fact, there is still a gun embrasure visible within one of the roadside walls, which would have been used when the Militia were conducting training exercises. This would have involved getting some very heavy cannons across the drill grounds and into position. These guns and

Guernsey Fire Station. (Soo Wellfair)

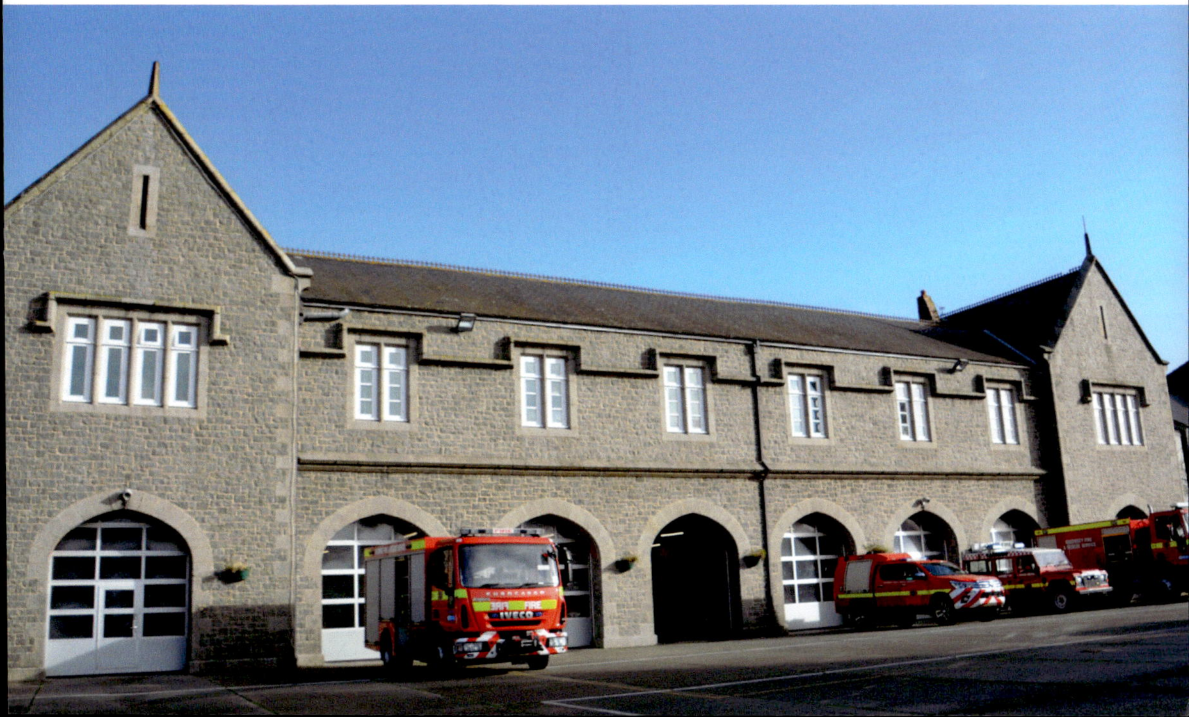

other equipment would have been stored at the Town Arsenal, which also served as barracks for soldiers and their families. There would also have been stables for military horses, so it was very much a multi-functional site.

In 1935 the building became home of the Guernsey Fire Brigade after they had relocated from a smaller building just around the corner, and enabled the brigade to be able to expand and meet the needs of twentieth-century fire fighting. Within a few years, the first full-time officer was employed in a system that had previously relied on volunteers, and this led to professional training and a more modern fire service which was re-named The Guernsey Fire and Rescue Service in 2005.

Much of the main building and yard are as they were back during the days of the Militia, although the site has been greatly expanded and adapted over the years to allow for the needs of the GFRS. The original, beautiful stone archways at the front of the building are still intact and form what are now the vehicle bays for the station. In 2010 it became necessary to modify the bays to enable the infrastructure to be able to withstand the weight of modern firefighting appliances. The original flagstone floor may have been beautiful, but it needed to be replaced with something more practical and safe. They were able to retain some of the flagstones in front of the bays, and the whole restoration at the time

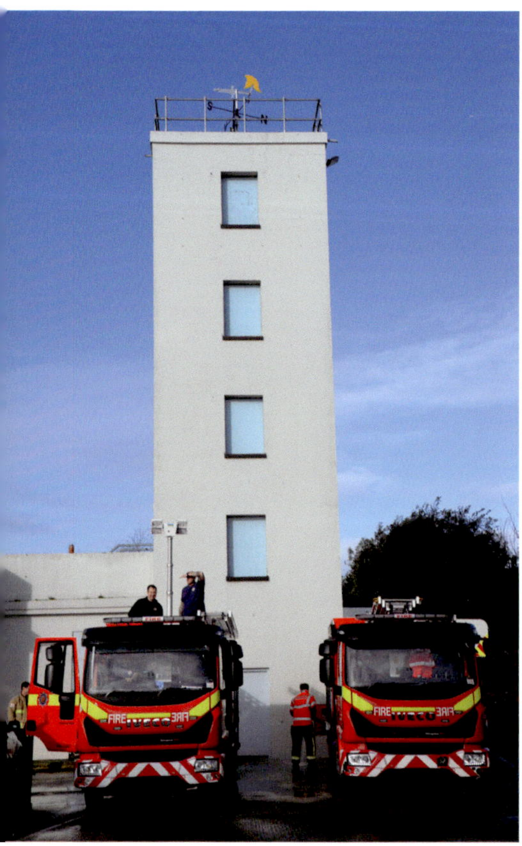

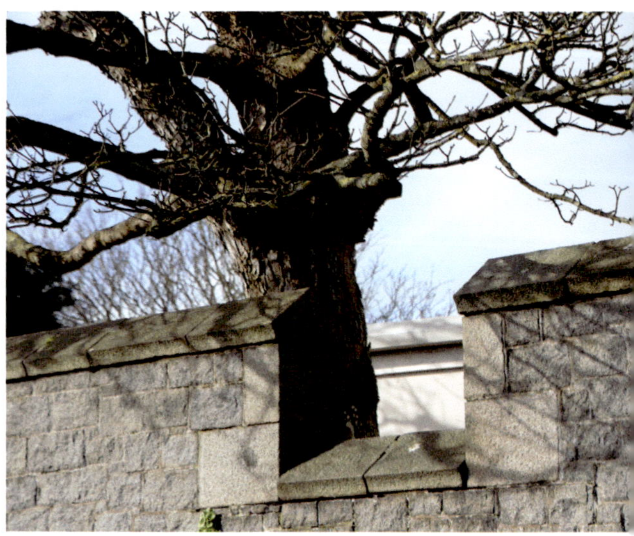

Above: Guernsey Militia gun embrasure. (Soo Wellfair)

Left: Training tower. (Soo Wellfair)

was very carefully carried out to ensure the aesthetics of this listed building were not compromised. An exciting contemporary feature of the site is the training tower and simulation area, which allows the team to train for a whole array of possible firefighting and rescue scenarios.

13. St Peter Port Constables' Office

This impressive townhouse is tucked away in a side street just off St Peter Port's High Street. Lefebvre Street can be found by walking through an attractive stone archway, which leads to a small courtyard surrounded by a real mixture of buildings, including the Constables' Office.

It was built in 1787 by the Bailiff of the island at the time, William Le Marchant. The Le Marchant family were a very well known, wealthy and prominent family in Guernsey, particularly in law, politics and the military. William himself had an

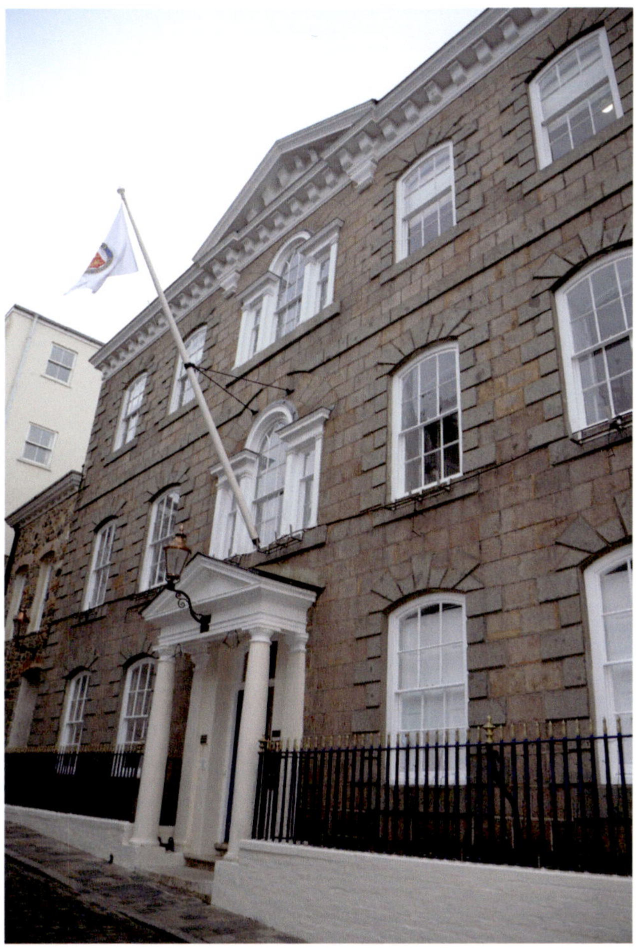

St Peter Port Constables' Office. (Soo Wellfair)

Eighteenth-century wallpaper. (Soo Wellfair)

illustrious career as both a Jurat of the Royal Court and as HM Receiver General before being appointed Bailiff between 1771 and 1800.

It is now the home of the St Peter Port Constables' Office and is where you will find the Parish Constables, who head up the Douzaine (much like a parish council). The Constables and the Douzaine are responsible for the administration of the parish. When the building was renovated in 2014, a large safe was moved, uncovering a large square or wallpaper which had been left there from when the building was the Le Marchant household. It is believed that the room which is now the main reception of the Constables' Office was once entirely decorated with this ornate wallpaper. It is thought to date back to 1780 and is made of a combination of parchment and linen and depicts scenes from the Book of Revelations. After the renovations, the safe was relocated and the wallpaper has been preserved behind glass.

14. Royal Court Buildings

The Royal Court can be located in St Peter Port, in the very heart of the town. It is an impressive grey granite building and is the home to not just the courtrooms and office of the Bailiff and other court officials, but also the meeting place of the island's government, the States of Deliberation. It is also where you will find the Greffe. The Greffe is essentially Guernsey's office for births, deaths and marriages, as well as conveyancing and much more besides. It is also where some of Guernsey's oldest and most historically significant documents are stored. Therefore, in UK terms, this one site encompasses the Guernsey equivalent of a courthouse, Parliament, archive and town hall, all in one.

The original architects of Guernsey's Royal Court buildings are unknown, but it is believed that the current court was completed in 1807, after it was moved from La Plaiderie (the Pleading Place). There were many structural and design issues with this new build, including problems with drainage and it was considered to be

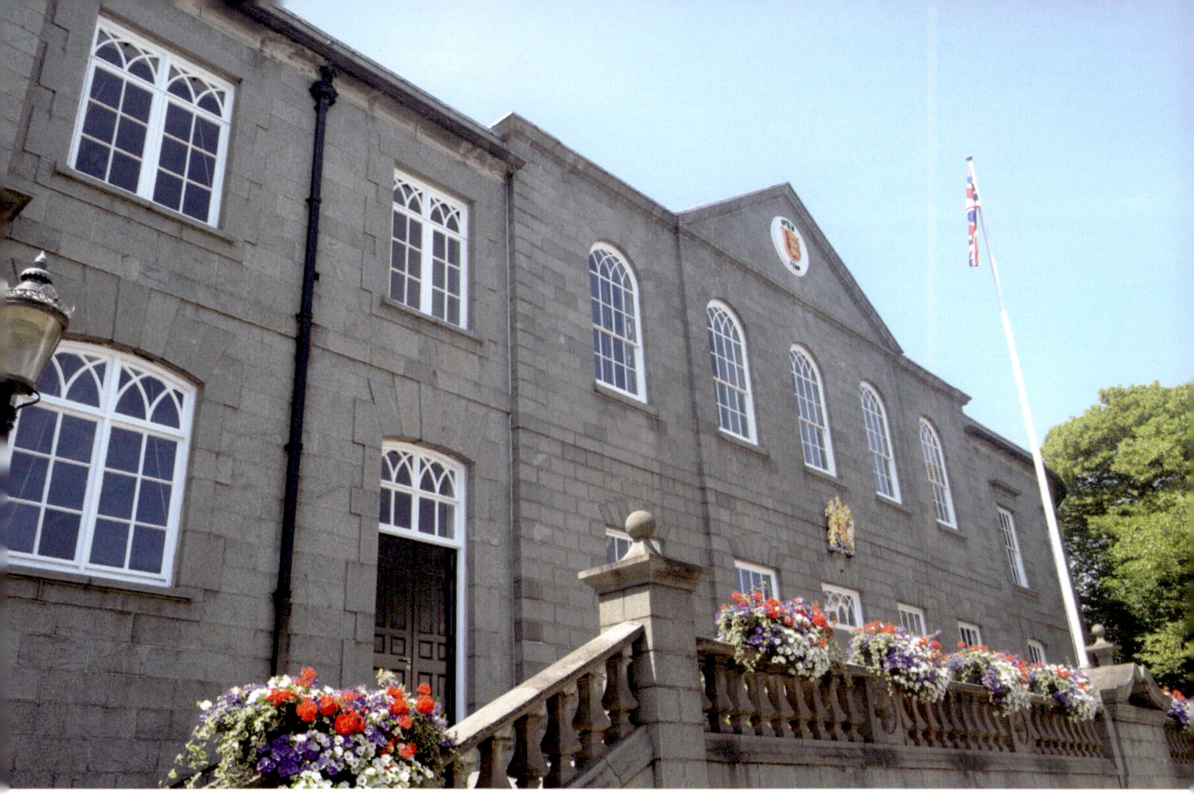

Above: Royal Court buildings. (Soo Wellfair)

Right: Wall taken from the former prison building. (Soo Wellfair)

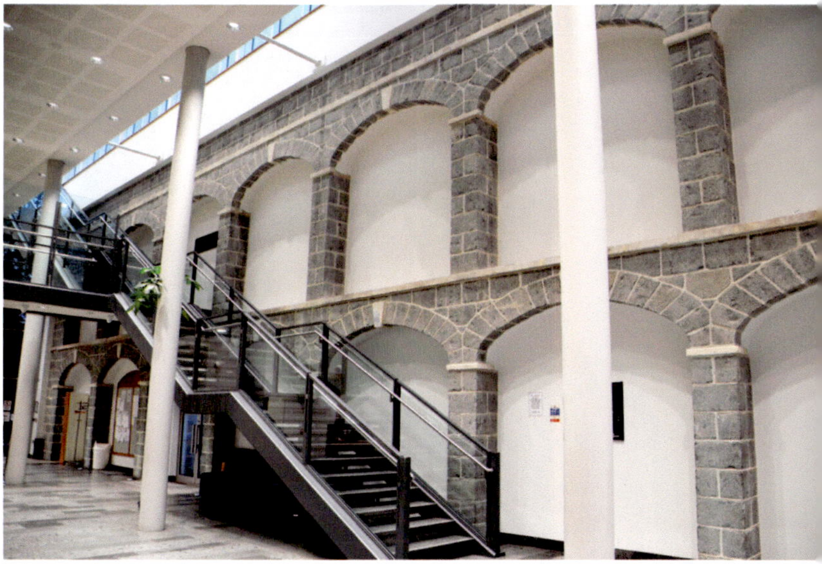

lacking in the privacy and opulence that a royal courthouse should have. Therefore, in 1822, architect John Wilson was drafted in to redesign and improve the site.

The Guernsey prison was once on the same site as the courthouse, with a bridge joining the two in the late nineteenth century. When the prison moved to a brand-new site in the north of the island, some of the prison architecture was incorporated into a redesign of the royal courts when the original prison was demolished.

15. Victoria Tower

In 1846 islanders were treated to a brief but exciting royal visit when Queen Victoria and Prince Albert came to Guernsey. Victoria Tower was built two years later in 1848 to both celebrate this historic moment and to hopefully encourage a return visit. The queen did in fact make a second visit to inspect the tower in 1851. Standing at around 100 feet tall, the tower sits 200 metres above sea level and is a prominent feature of the St Peter Port skyline, particularly when viewed from the harbour. It can even be seen from the other side of the island on a clear day. This impressive structure was constructed using mostly beautiful, pink granite from Cobo on the west coast and cost approximately £2,000. This was considered rather expensive at the time and was largely funded by public donations, which were needed to help cover the lofty costs of the project. Buried in the foundations is a time capsule, containing a selection of coins from both Guernsey and England. The island's most skilled stonemasons would have been employed to create the monument and their skills shown off by using the most up-to-date and artistic techniques of the time.

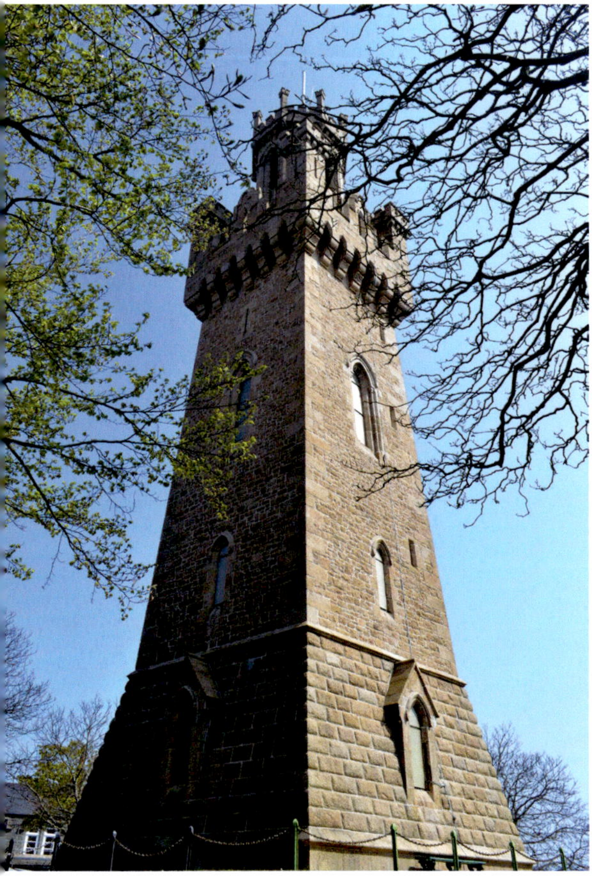

Left: Victoria Tower. (Soo Wellfair)

Below: Spiral staircase, Victoria Tower. (Soo Wellfair)

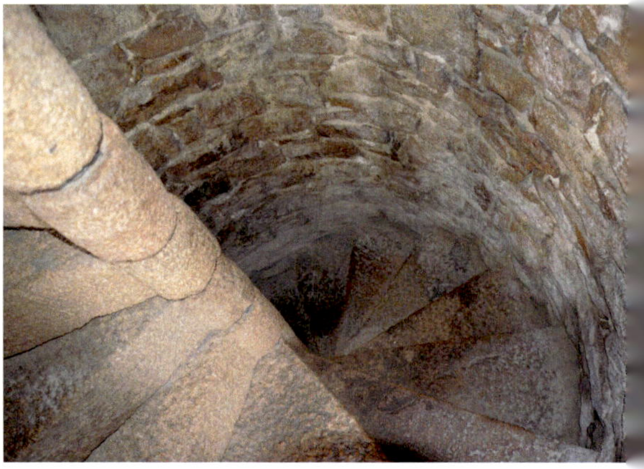

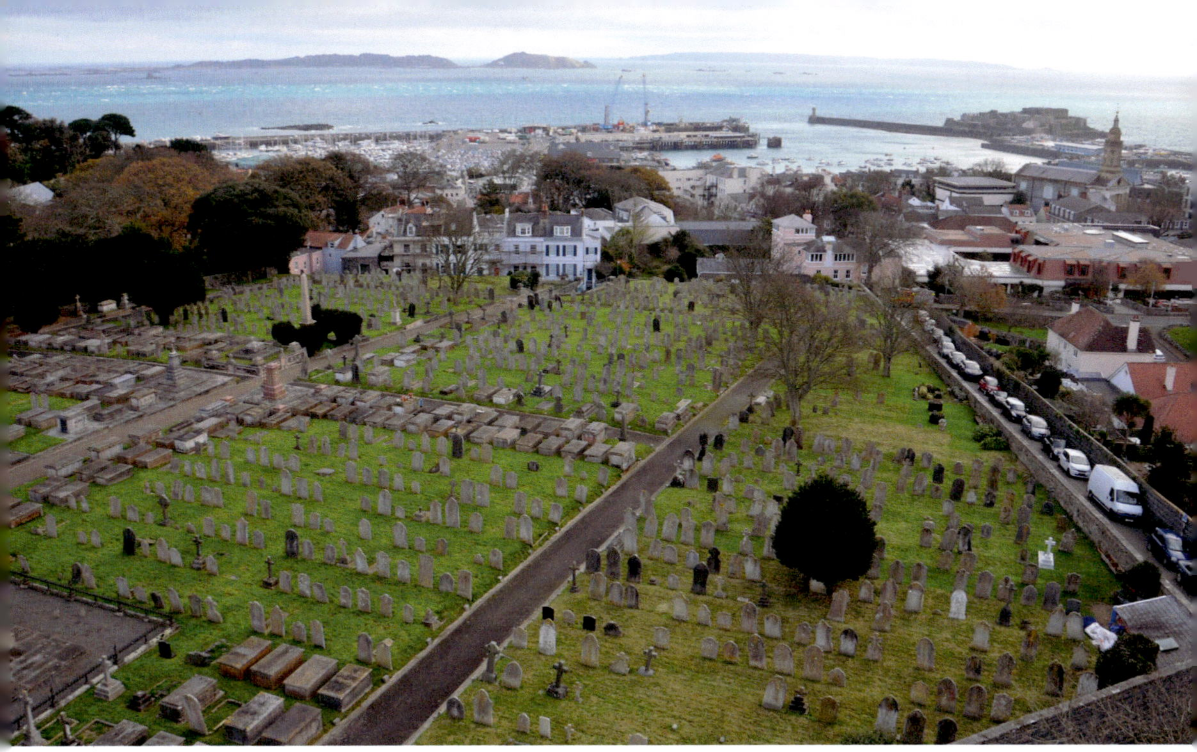

The view from Victoria Tower. (Soo Wellfair)

It is believed that the French writer Victor Hugo and his mistress Juliette Drouet would secretly meet inside Victoria Tower, and somewhere in the pink granite you will find their intertwined initials engraved.

The gardens surrounding the tower are also where you will find two rather interesting pieces of military artillery: two large German First World War guns which were thought to have made their way over to Guernsey in the early 1920s. It was not unusual for cannons to be displayed in the gardens, as the town arsenal was situated just across the road (now the Guernsey Fire Station). The two guns in the gardens today were originally a set of four. After the Second World War broke out, two were scrapped and the remaining two were hastily buried in 1940, just before Guernsey was occupied. However, they remained underground until 1978 when they were excavated, restored and put back on display in their current location.

Although the tower is kept locked, the key can be taken out on loan from the Guernsey Museum at Candie Gardens. Visitors are able to climb the ninety-nine steps up the internal spiral staircase. This leads to a viewing platform at the top of the tower, which boasts amazing panoramic views of St Peter Port and beyond.

16. Guernsey Police Headquarters

Situated along a narrow and steep town road named Hospital Lane, the home of the Guernsey Police is a striking building with a fascinating history. Built in the mid-eighteenth century, it was originally named the House of Charity and

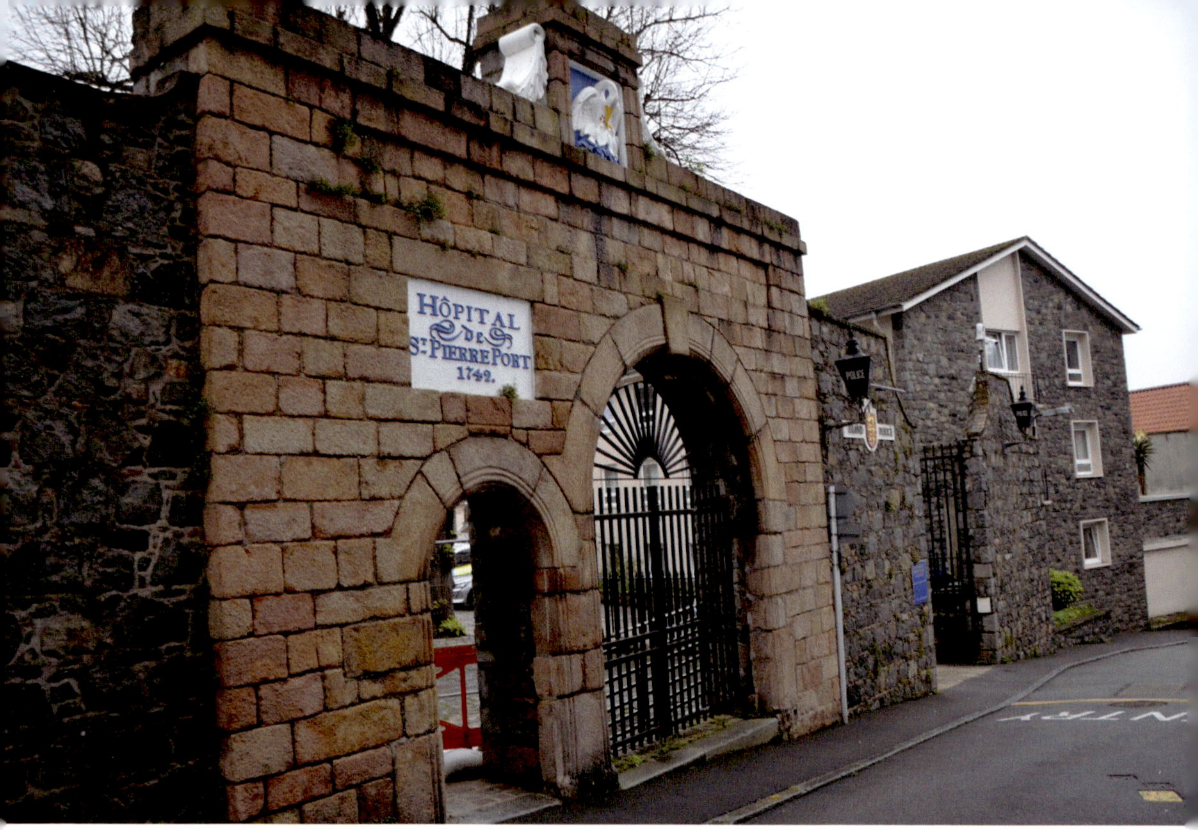

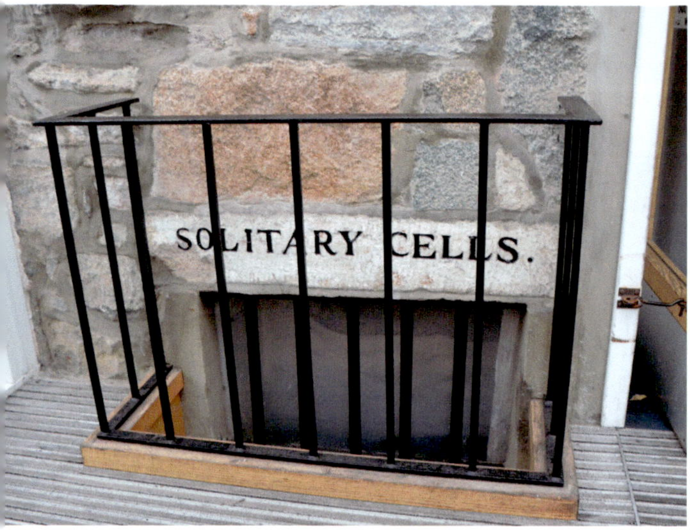

Above: Police station/former hospital entrance. (Soo Wellfair)

Left: Solitary confinement cells. (Soo Wellfair)

was set up as a workhouse for the poor. As the building has been modified and modernised much over the years, there is very little to remind us of its original purpose. However, downstairs in the basement of the building you can still find the workhouse's original solitary confinement cells with their original doors which are now used for storage. The building has been extended over the years and was used as the Town Hospital for some time.

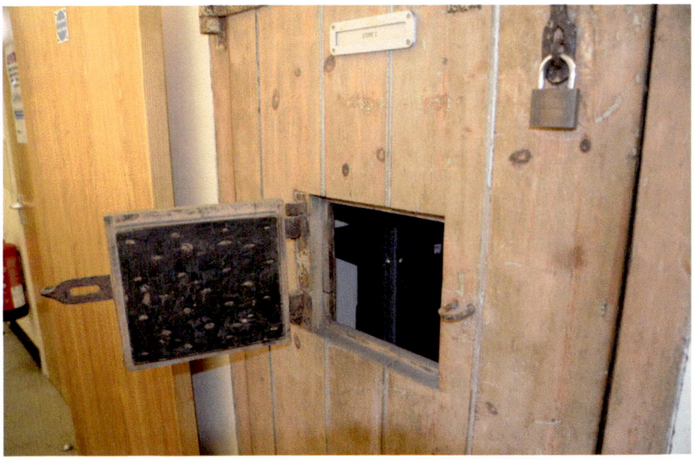

Old cell rooms.
(Soo Wellfair)

The large archway which acts as an entrance to the paved courtyard in front of the building was installed when the Town Hospital was opened. It was in fact moved from the nearby area of L'Hyvreuse when the land of a former estate there was sold for use as a Royal Militia parade ground and the archway deemed too narrow for purpose. At that point the emblem of the pelican was created and added to the archway. The pelican is widely accepted as a symbol of charity and self-sacrifice and possibly depicts a 'Pelican in her Piety', a religious allegory well known at the time. In 1993 the building became the new home of the Guernsey Police, who had moved location from just up the road. In 2020 the Guernsey Police celebrated their 100-year anniversary and this building is the main headquarters of the force and a base for all major policing departments, including the ordnance disposal team and the police dog section, which has its own on-site training ground. The Guernsey Police also share the building with the Joint Emergency Services Control Centre, which deals with calls to all emergency services in the Bailiwick of Guernsey.

17. States Building, North Plantation

This beautiful, large, grey granite building dominates the St Peter Port seafront in an area known as the North Plantation. As well as being an impressive structure, it is often adorned with colourful flower boxes and throughout the year is swathed in greenery.

It was built in 1911 to serve as a States Office for the harbour. As St Peter Port Harbour had recently expanded it was deemed necessary that a newer, bigger office was needed for the collection of harbour duties. This site was chosen as it was perfectly located between the older and newer sections of the harbour.

The foundation stone was laid in 1911, and the office was opened to the public in September 1913. The building is mostly made of local granodiorite, quarried in

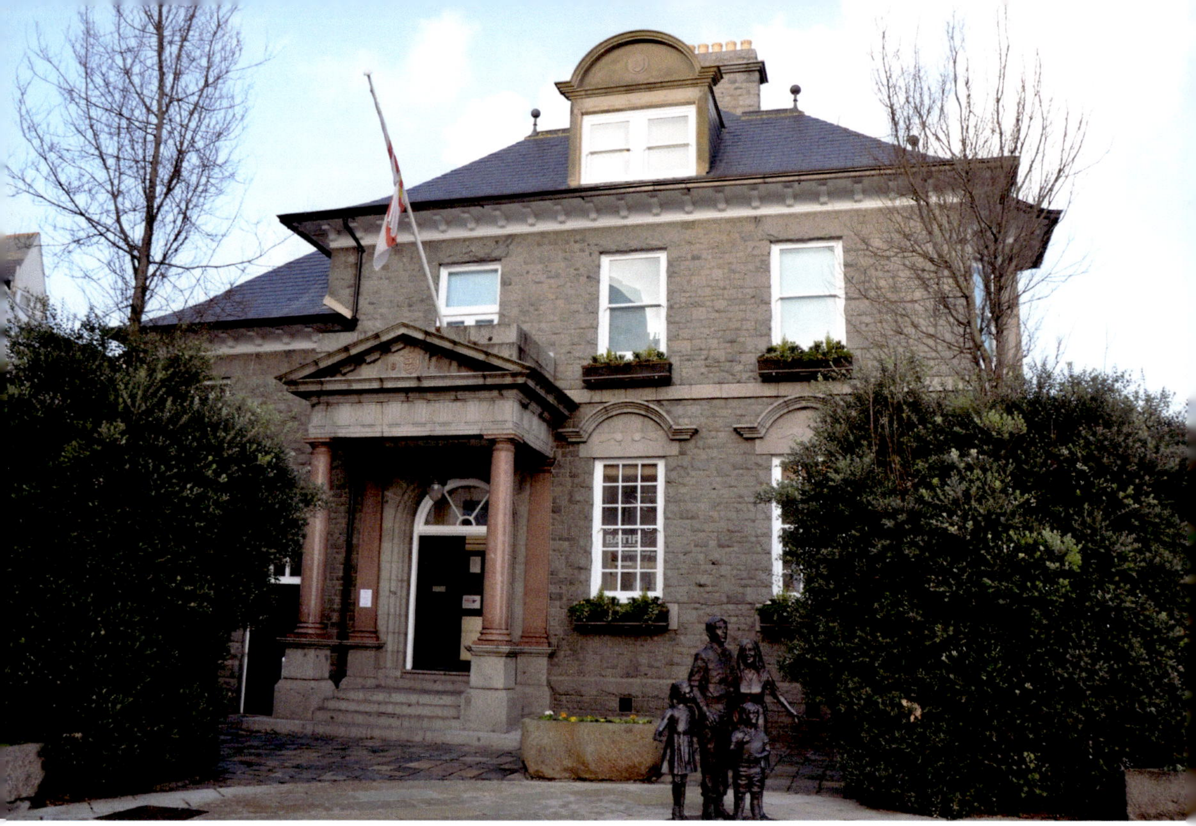

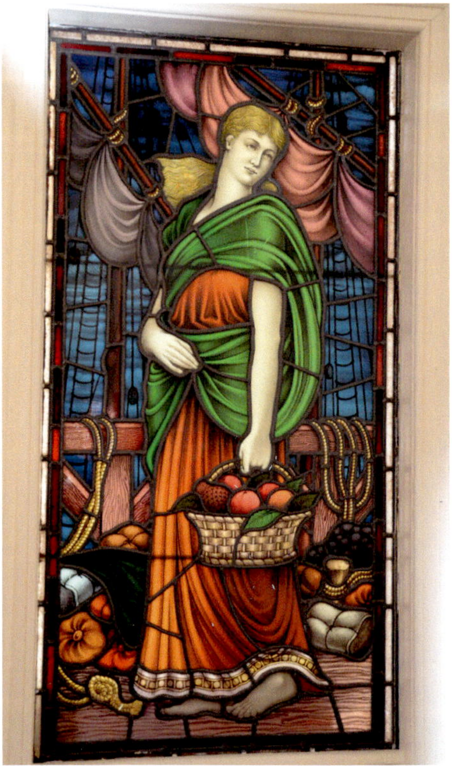

Above: States building, North Plantation. (Soo Wellfair)

Left: Stained-glass window celebrating Guernsey industry. (Soo Wellfair)

the northern end of the island. However, the ornate pillars in the front porchway were made with red granite from Aberdeen, as a softer stone was required to achieve the look needed. Concrete was also used extensively, which was quite unusual for the time period. In fact, it is considered one of the earliest examples of a granite building incorporating concrete in Guernsey.

The building is still States owned and has had various departments operating from the premises, including the Guernsey Information Centre, Guernsey Post and the Guernsey Arts Commission. There are plans for the building to be transformed into a visitor centre, celebrating the life and work of Victor Hugo.

Many of the building's original features remain, including the stained-glass windows in the hallway, which depict industry and commerce in Guernsey.

18. Island Archives

In one of St Peter Port's more elevated areas, sitting proudly on the site of a former ancient fort named the Tour de Beauregard, you will find the Island Archives building. It is more commonly known locally as St Barnabas Church, despite not having been used as a place of worship since the 1930s.

Back in the late nineteenth century, it was felt that a second church was needed in St Peter Port as the Town Church did not meet the needs of the whole community. The first stone of the new church was laid by the Bailiff, Sir Peter Stafford-Carey,

Island Archives/former St Barnabas Church. (Soo Wellfair)

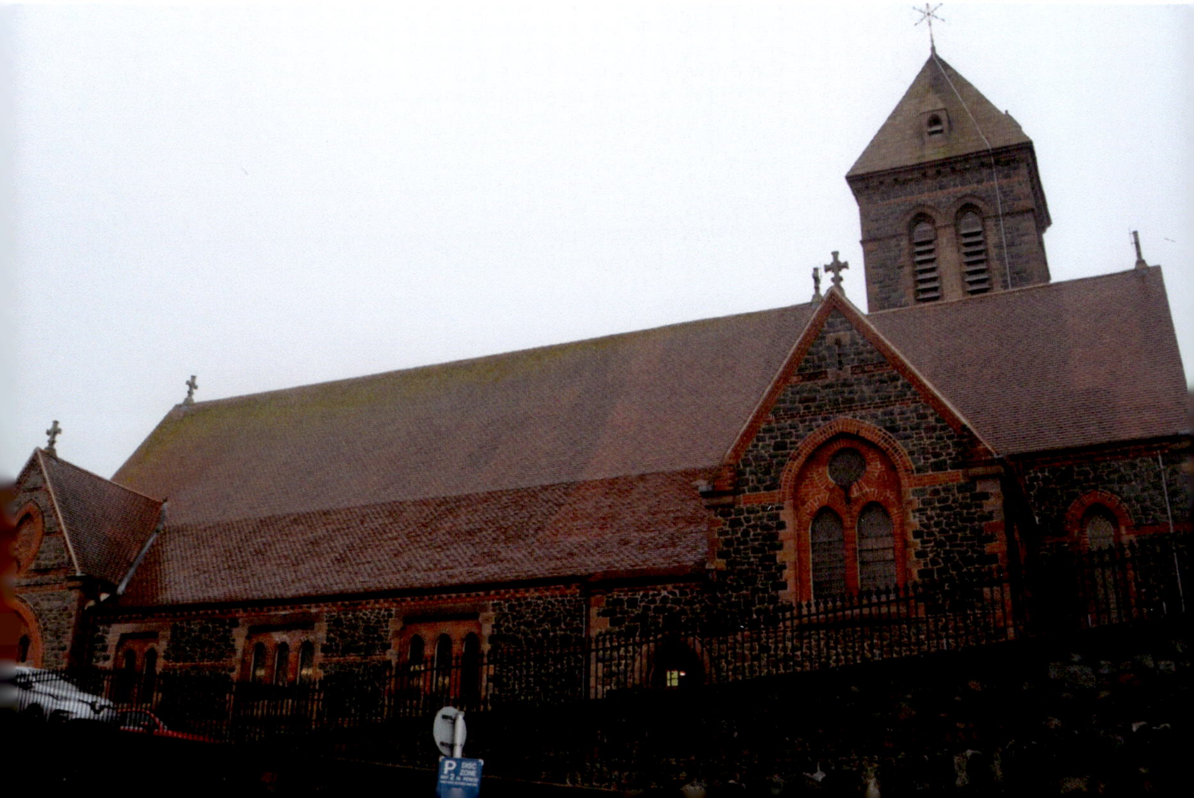

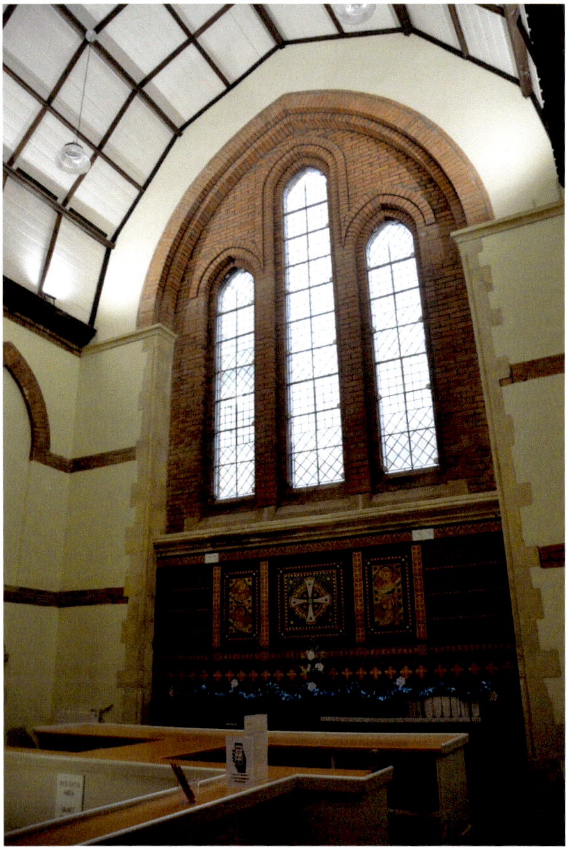

Research room. (Soo Wellfair)

on 11 June 1872, which incidentally was St Barnabus Day. St Barnabas was known for helping the poor, so it was a very fitting dedication indeed. The building was constructed using a combination of local pink and blue granite with some red brickwork and was built in the Gothic style at a cost of £3,000. By the beginning of the 1930s the building was no longer being used as a church due to poor attendance and the building falling into disrepair. It was handed over from the church to the States of Guernsey and was utilised in many ways over the years. For some time it was used as a soup kitchen and later became the Lukis and Island Museum, housing the vast collection of local archaeologist Frederick Lukis. When the museum moved in the 1970s the building was used mostly for storage but was also largely left unused for many years. In 2003 it was decided that the protected building should be renovated and transformed into the Island Archives at a cost of just shy of £3,000,000. The Island Archives was opened in 2006 and houses an enormous amount of States records, as well as historical and family documents, some of which date back as early as the fourteenth century. Whilst the restoration project involved many modifications to ensure the building met the modern needs of the Island Archives, such as environmentally controlled strongrooms, many of the original features of the church have been retained.

19. Priaulx Library

The Priaulx Library was originally named Candie House and was built as a private residence in the 1780s. It is likely to have been built on the site of another building and was possibly partially rebuilt or extended when it came into the ownership of Peter Mourant, a local merchant and businessman. The house first came into the hands of the Priaulx family in 1830, when it was purchased by Joshua Priaulx and later sold to his brother Osmond de Beauvoir Priaulx. For some time the house was rented to the Bailiff of Guernsey, Sir Peter Stafford Carey, until he passed away in 1886. It was at this point that plans to transform the house into a public library were put into effect. Osmond de Beauvoir Priaulx gifted the house, his extensive book collection and a sizable amount of money to Guernsey, on the condition that it was to be transformed into the island's first free public library. The renovations were extensive with work including having the entire roof replaced and the top floor raised by a foot. Queen Anne gables and dormer windows were also added to create a roomy attic space. Most of the grounds were sold at a peppercorn rate to the States, to be opened as public gardens.

The Priaulx Library has been open to the public since 1889 and is now highly regarded as Guernsey's primary resource for local studies and family history research. The library has an extensive collection of books, records, newspapers and photographs and regularly hosts local exhibitions.

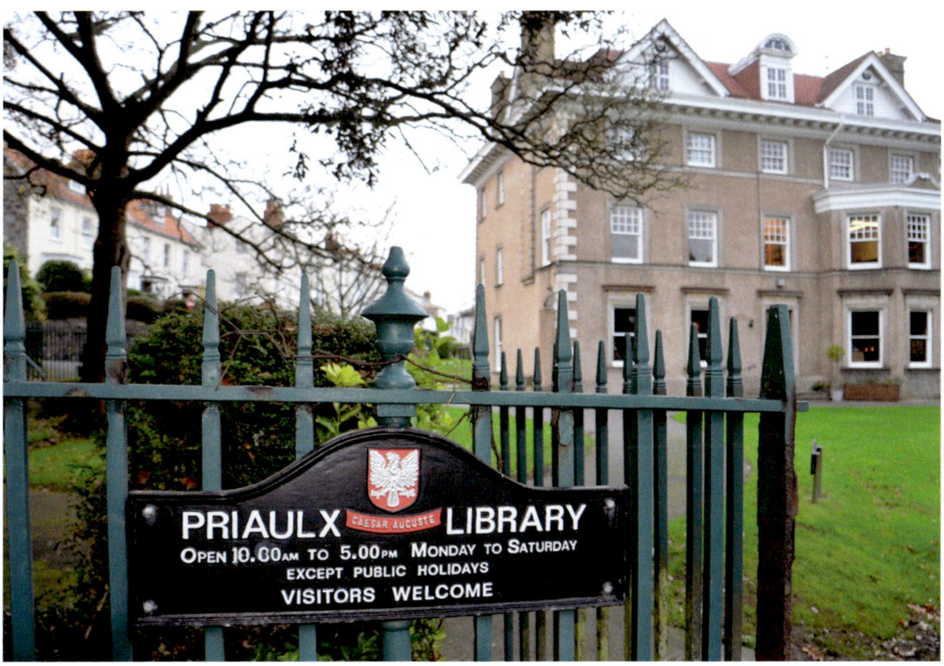

Priaulx Library. (Soo Wellfair)

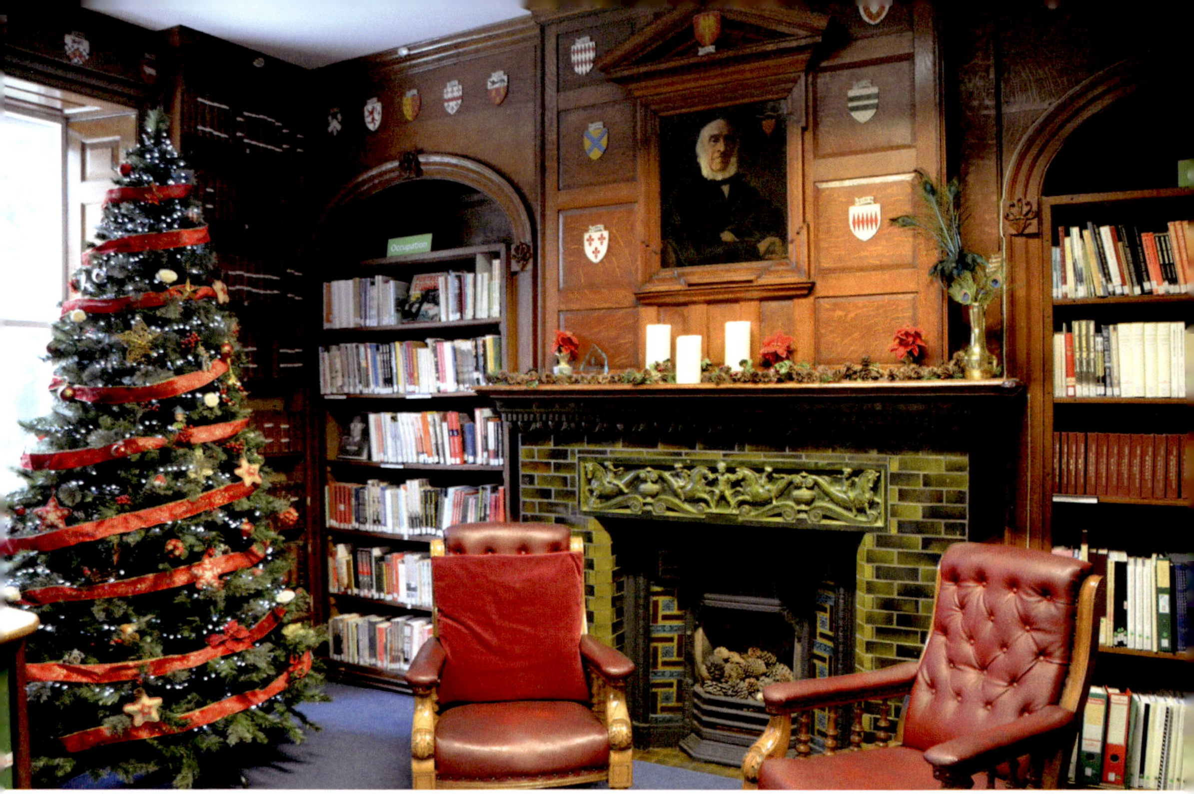

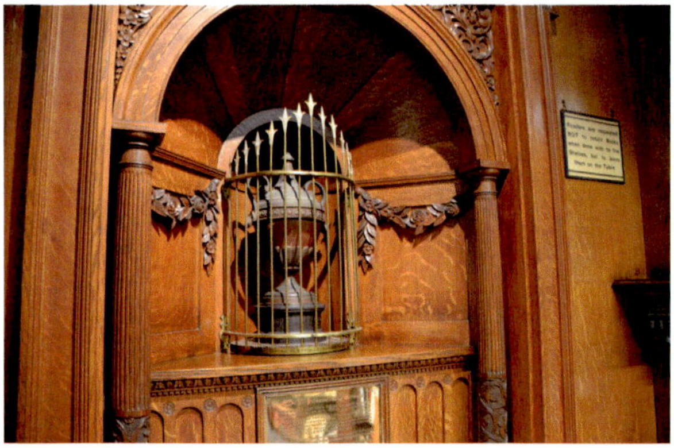

Above: Study area. (Soo Wellfair)

Left: Ashes of Osmond de Beauvoir Priaulx. (Soo Wellfair)

Osmond de Beauvoir Priaulx had insisted that the library be simply named Candie Library, but it became known as the Priaulx Library and the name stuck. In fact, the name is not the only reminder of the library's generous benefactor, as the ashes of Osmond de Beauvoir Priaulx are on display in a beautiful decorative urn.

20. Fort George

Fort George was once a vast defensive complex, built to accommodate the increasing number of British soldiers being billeted on the island as a response to the ongoing threat of French invasion in the late eighteenth century. Work began in 1780 and was officially opened and named after King George III in 1812. It was designed to act as the main military headquarters for the British army in Guernsey and also acted as barracks for the various regiments garrisoned there and also provided training facilities for the Royal Guernsey Militia and later, the Light Infantry.

It was an impressive stronghold, heavily armoured and built on top of the most elevated part of St Peter Port, overlooking the harbour. At one point the fort was thought to have had around forty guns (mostly cannons) in situ, with further support from nearby gun batteries. Fort George was taken over by the occupying forces during the Second World War and renamed Stützpunkt Georgefest. During this time the fort was greatly reinforced and a Freya radar was installed.

The States of Guernsey purchased the land from the Crown in 1958, and in the 1960s it was passed onto property developers who constructed a luxury housing estate within the walls of the original fort. Still named Fort George, this is still one of the most sought-after housing areas in Guernsey, mostly down to the unrivalled views and location. Much of the fort is still very much in place – from the grand archway that leads into the estate, to the thick walls that make up the perimeter.

Within the grounds of Fort George, you will also find a beautifully maintained cemetery nestled amongst the residential areas. The Fort George Military Ce

Fort George entrance. (Soo Wellfair)

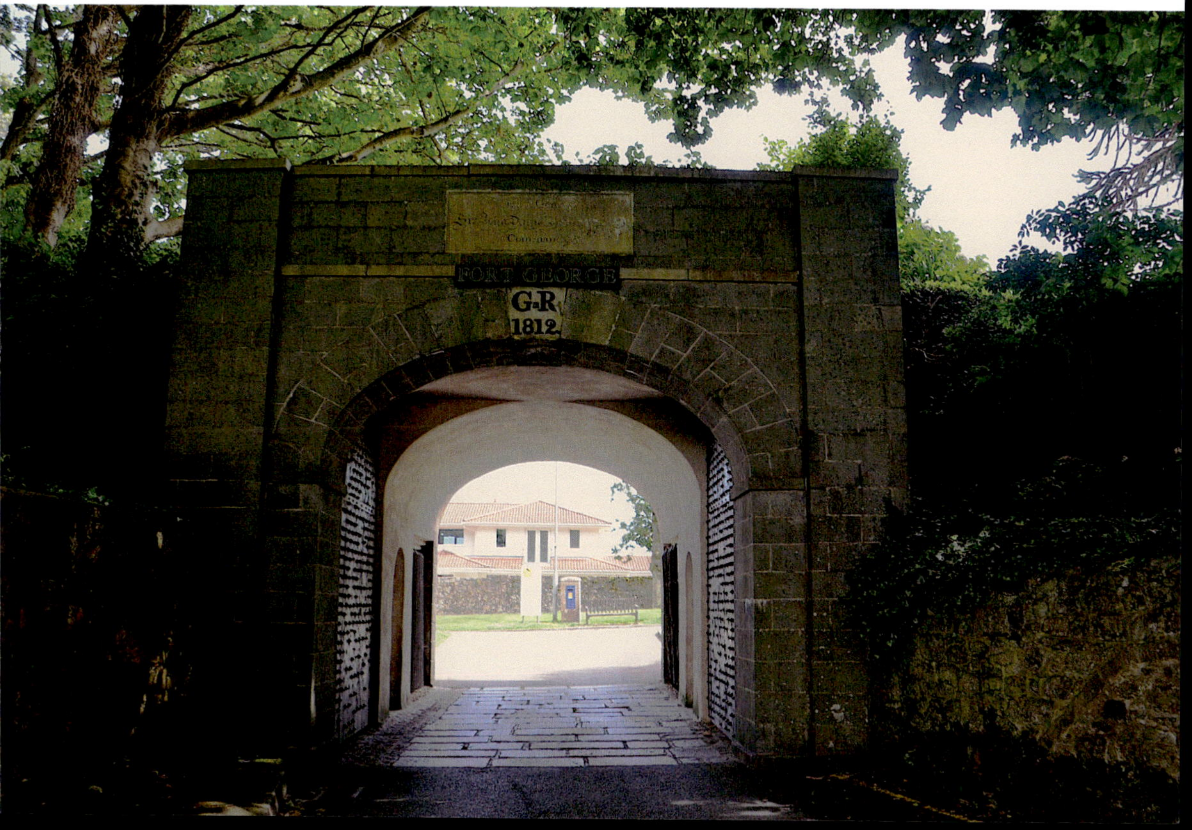

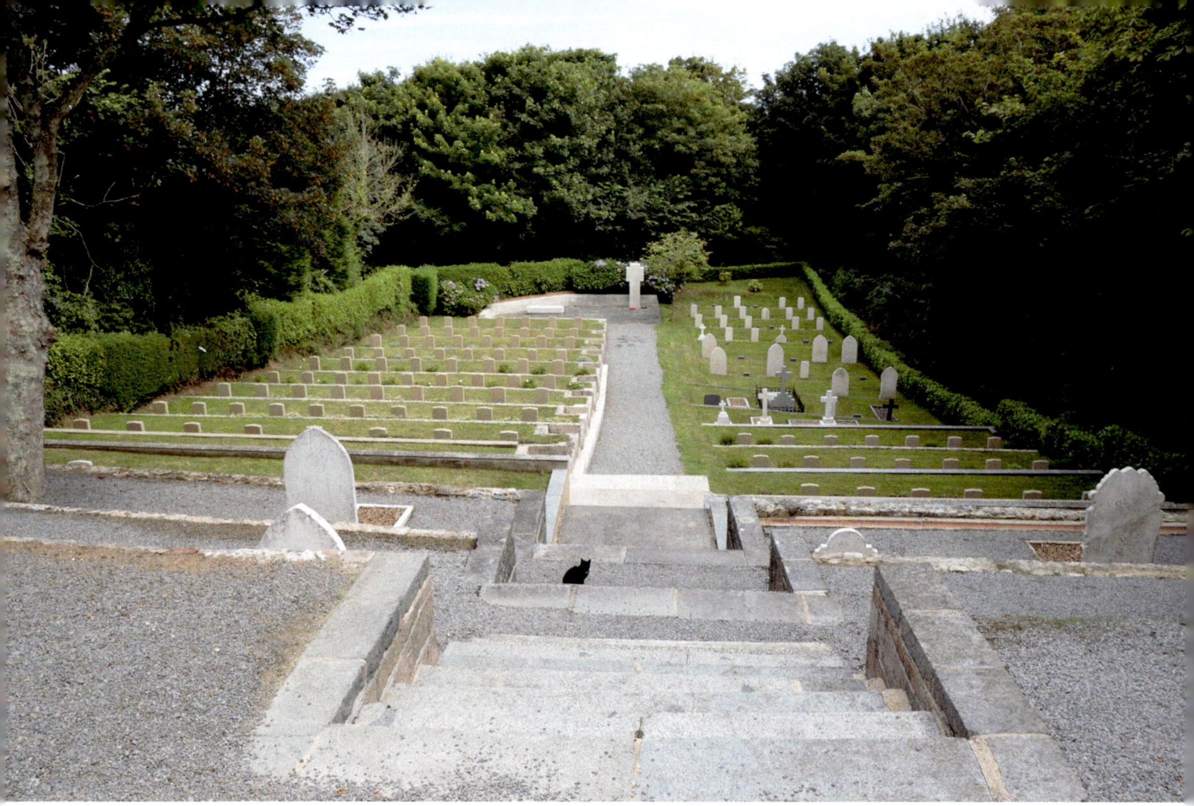

Military cemetery. (Soo Wellfair)

Benedictine forms metery is the burial place of members of the British Armed Forces who died in the Bailiwick of Guernsey during the nineteenth and twentieth centuries, as well as 111 German graves from the Second World War. It acts as both a final resting place and war memorial.

21. Vale Church

The parish church of St Michel du Valle can be found in Guernsey's most northerly parish, Vale. Prior to 1806 the very top of the Vale, known as the Clos du Valle, was separated from the rest of Guernsey by a stretch of water called the Braye Du Valle, which split the island into two at high tide. The Vale Parish Church once sat right on the edge of this tidal inlet, before the area was drained and Guernsey became one island. The north of Guernsey is also where you will find a large number of prehistoric sites, so it comes as no surprise that there are the remains of a Neolithic passage grave in the churchyard, as well as an example of an ancient menhir or standing stone which was later marked with the sign of a cross.

Vale Church is one of Guernsey's oldest places of worship, being on the site of a former priory, built for Benedictine monks from Mont St Michel in the tenth century. The church itself, which was dedicated in the twelfth century, still has elements that would suggest monastic influence, which is unique in Guernsey.

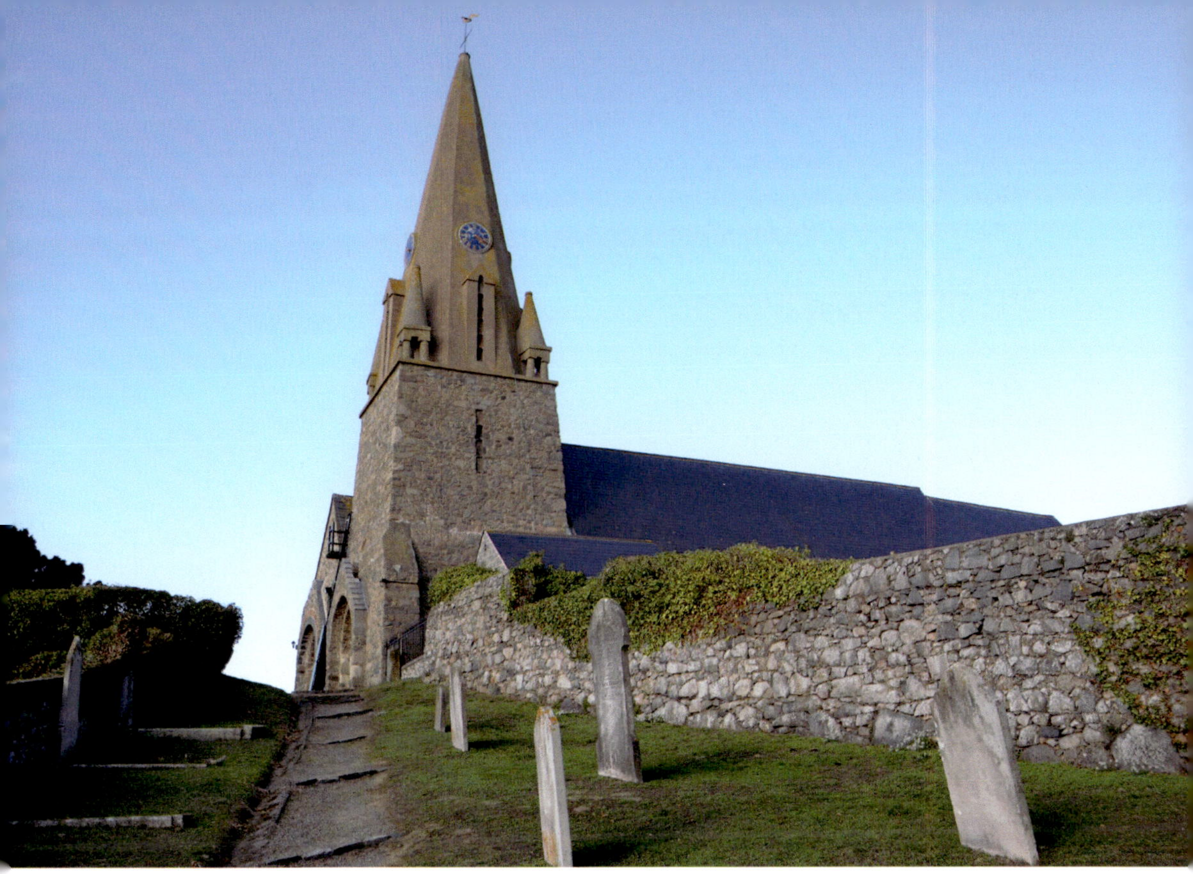

Above: Vale Church. (Soo Wellfair)

Below left: Sea Witch grave and memorial. (Soo Wellfair)

Below right: Font and bell-ringing area. (Soo Wellfair)

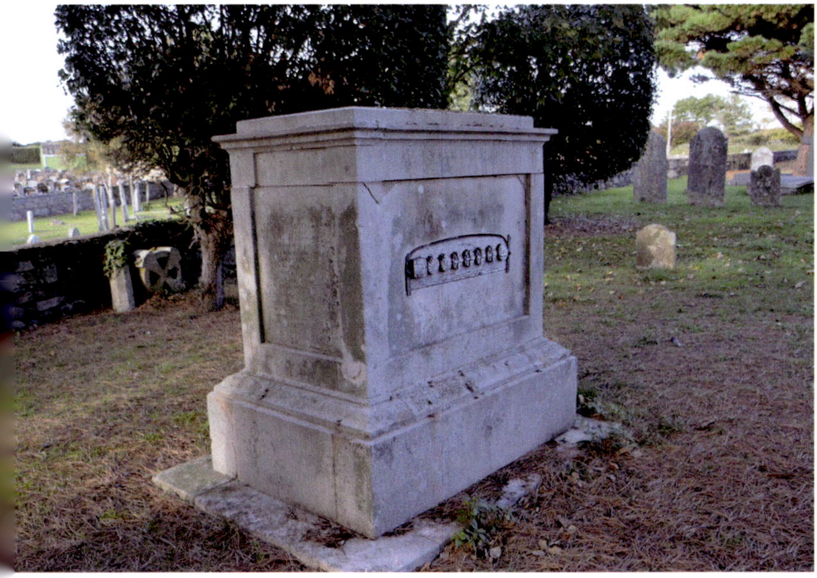

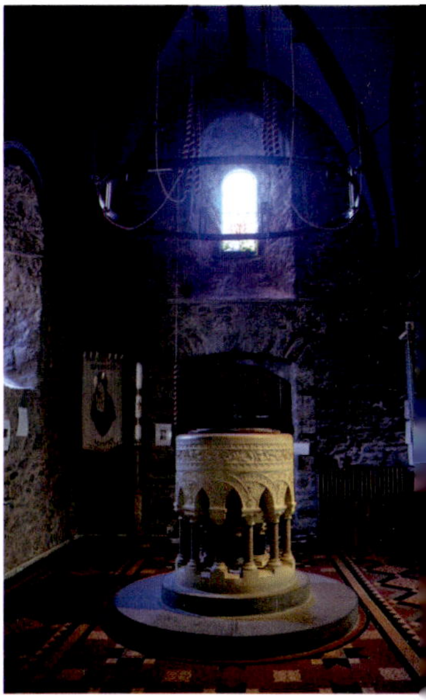

The buttresses of the priory are still standing and now form part of a small community hall on the grounds of the church.

The clock of Vale Church is quite unique in Guernsey. It was installed in 1897 to celebrate Queen Victoria's diamond jubilee and is the only church clock on the island to play the Westminster chimes. There is a set of six bells dating back to the late nineteenth century, when they replaced an existing peel of three medieval bells. The bell ringers in Vale have quite an interesting location to conduct their bell ringing. Whilst they were originally based in the church tower, the bell ropes now hang down into the baptistry and the ringers stand around the font to ring the bells.

A notable burial plot in the churchyard, also acts as a memorial of the sinking of the *Sea Witch* ship in 1848. Eight of the ship's crew lost their lives when the ship was wrecked nearby and they were buried at Vale Church. The tomb that marks the grave was embellished, using a piece of timber taken from the wreck. This piece of African oak is engraved with eight symbols, representing each lost crew member.

22. Vale Castle

In the north of the island, overlooking the parishes of Vale and St Sampson, you will find Vale Castle. It is thought that the castle was built in the late fourteenth or early fifteenth century as a place of refuge in times of invasion. Vale Castle stands in an area once known as the Clos du Valle, which up until the early nineteenth century was actually separated from the rest of Guernsey by a stretch of water known as the Braye du Valle. Although the castle was unlikely to have been intended for military purposes, it has been regularly garrisoned over the centuries. It is a D-shaped fortification with six D-shaped towers around the outer walls, which have been filled in for many years. The main entrance to the castle is made up of three archways, all slightly different. There is also an obvious gap where there would have once been a portcullis, although there is no evidence of there ever being a drawbridge. Whilst none of the main interior buildings remain, there are some reminders of when the castle was inhabited, including what is left of the castle's only fresh water source; a small well. During the First World War, barracks were built, which later became social housing for many years but were demolished soon after the Second World War. One of the most unusual features of Vale Castle is a tiny cemetery dating back to 1928, created when the remains from a nearby cemetery were reinterred, when the original cemetery was purchased by a nearby quarry.

The castle was taken over during the Second World War and there are many bunkers and gun positions still visible, as well as some that have become hidden, as nature has reclaimed the area.

Today, Vale Castle is a heritage site, accessible to the public and free to explore. It has also become a popular venue for music concerts, open-air theatre productions and weddings.

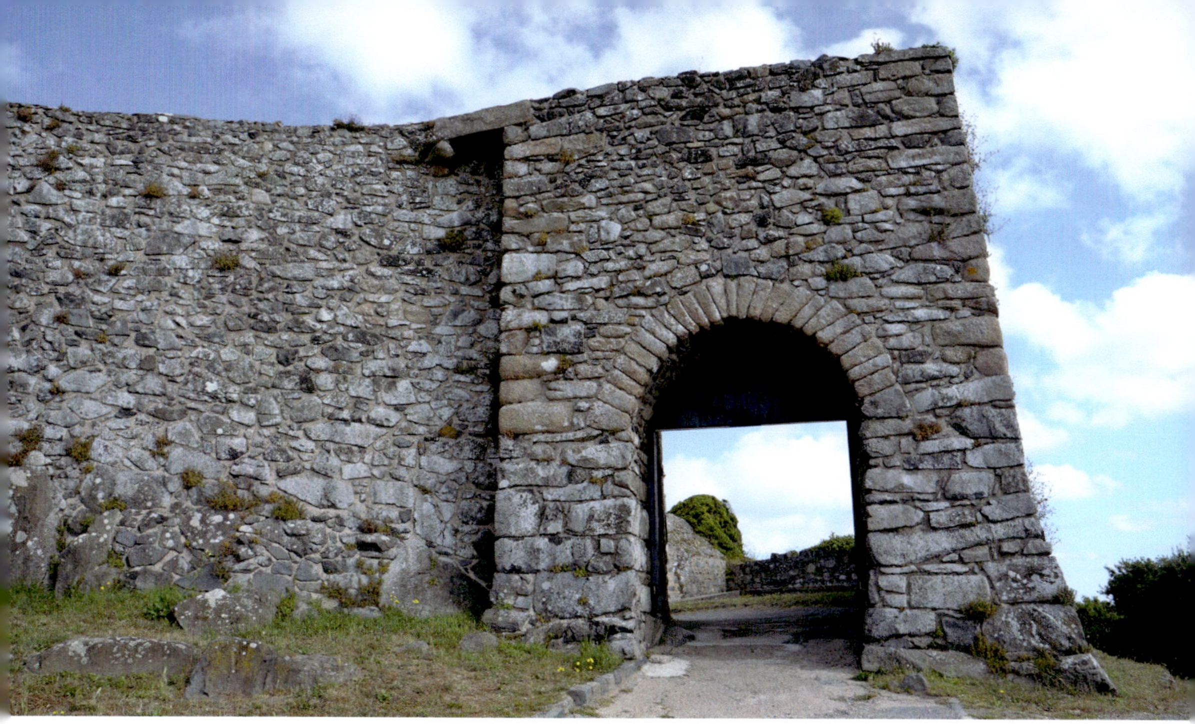

Above: Vale Castle. (Soo Wellfair)

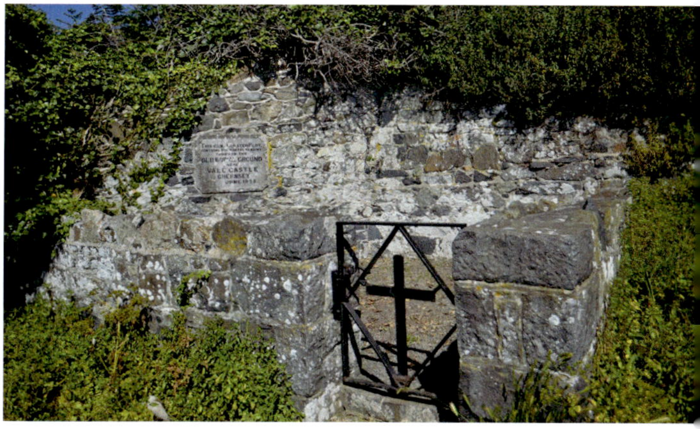

Right: Cemetery, 1928.
(Soo Wellfair)

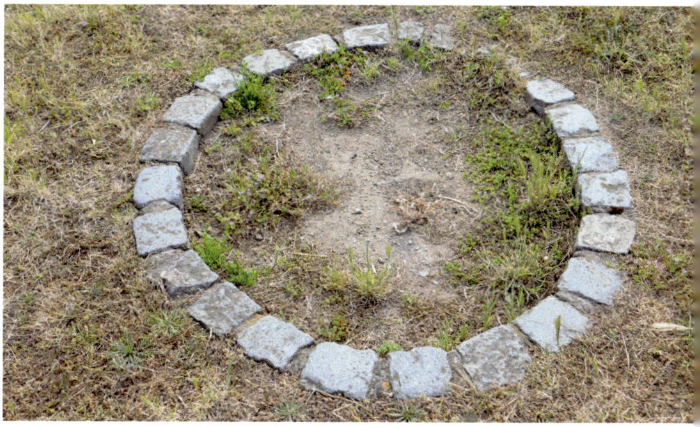

Remains of a well. (Soo Wellfair)

22. Fort Le Marchant

Fort Le Marchant can be found along Guernsey's rocky and tempestuous north coast. It is believed that a fort has existed from the site since at least the seventeenth century, although it's likely to have been quite a small fortification and was later expanded and reinforced. It was originally called Fort L'Angle and renamed in the early nineteenth century after the Lieutenant Bailiff at the time, Eleazar Le Marchant. At this time six twenty-four-pounder guns were installed on traversing platforms to defend the nearby bays. The guns have long since gone, although you can still see what is left of their platforms today. Victorian barracks were built around the fort

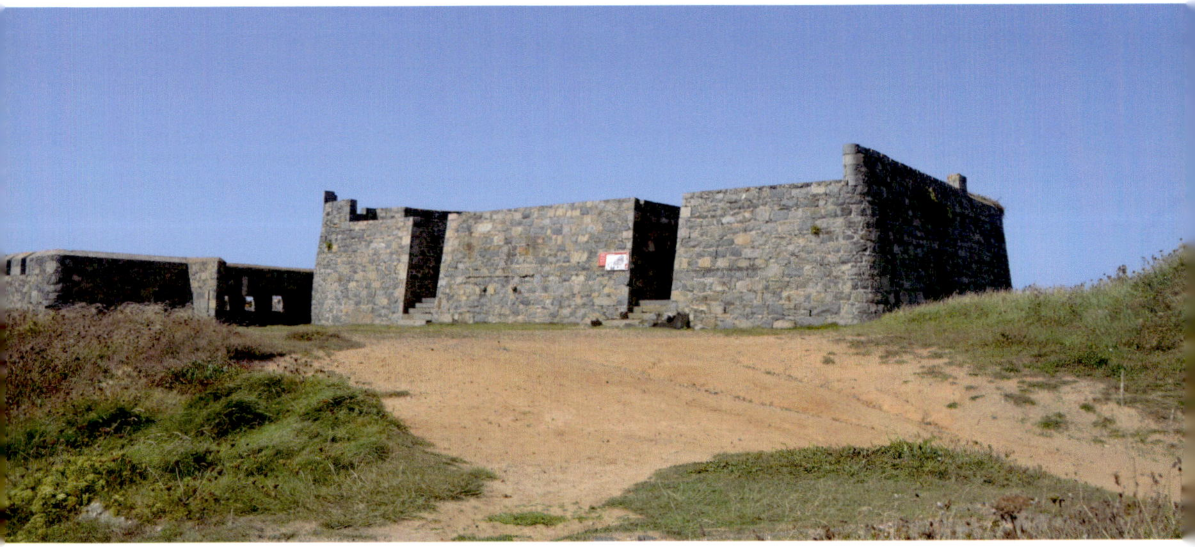

Above: Fort Le Marchant. (Soo Wellfair)

Below: Rifle range markers. (Soo Wellfair)

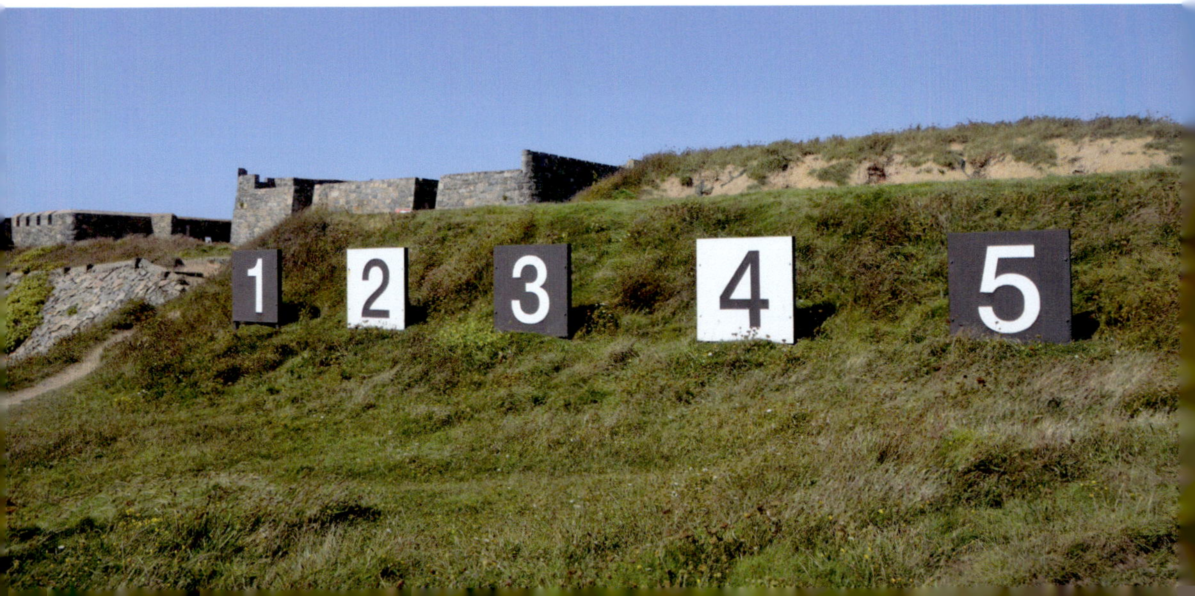

in the 1850s, which were later used when soldiers were garrisoned there during the First World War. During the Second World War they sustained significant damage and by the 1960s were in a terrible state of disrepair and demolished in 1971. It was at this point that the defensive ditches surrounding the fort were also filled in.

Today, the remains of the fort are considered a historic site and can be visited by the public. It is also the home of the Guernsey Rifle Club. The club was founded in 1871 and has been based at the fort since 1955, with access to the site restricted during shooting times.

23. Vale Mill

Windmills were once quite a common site in Guernsey, with up to twelve of them dotted around the island. Looking over the parish of Vale, you will find Vale Mill. The mill was originally built around 1770 and was made of wood. Within a hundred years the wooden mill had been replaced by a sturdier granite structure, and it worked as a mill for many years. The mill had fallen into disuse by the time it was taken over by the German army during the Second World War. The occupying forces stripped the mill of all interior equipment and removed the sails. It was originally used by the Seenotdienst, the German sea rescue service but later became an observation tower and range finder. To enable this, three storeys were added to the top of the mill, complete with 360-degree slots for observing and a painted panorama. These concrete floors were then clad with granite and a fake domed roof (ogee cap) was added to the top level to disguise

Vale Mill and quarry. (Soo Wellfair)

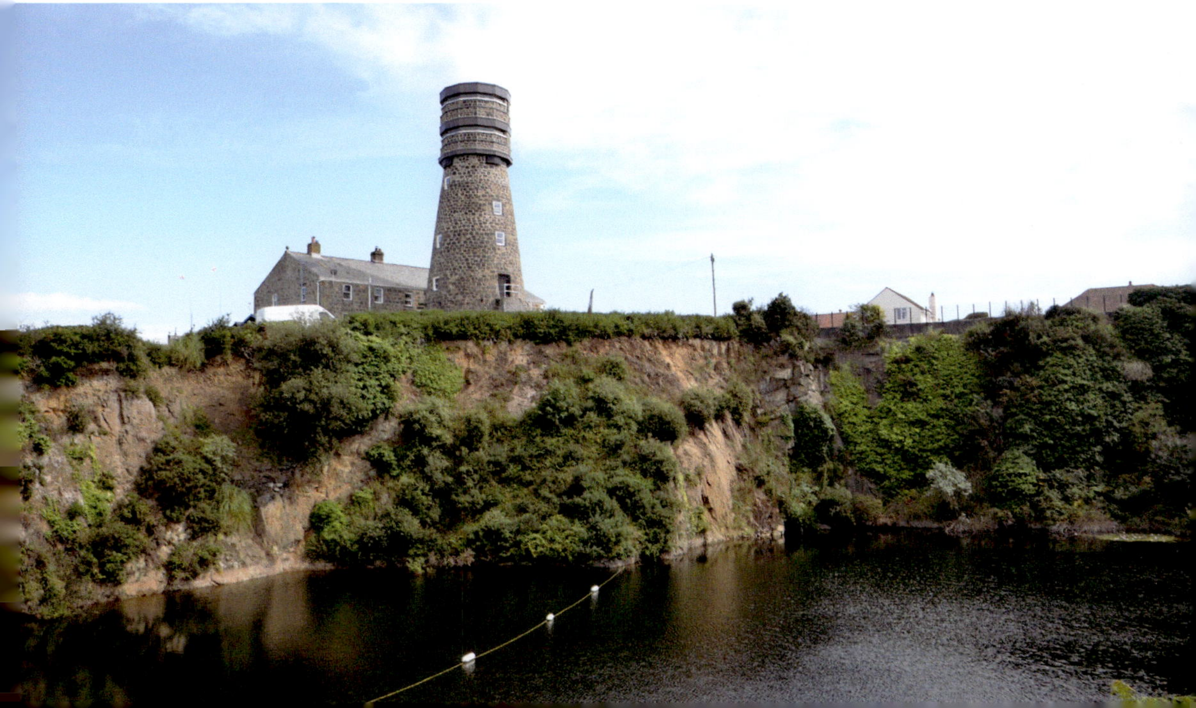

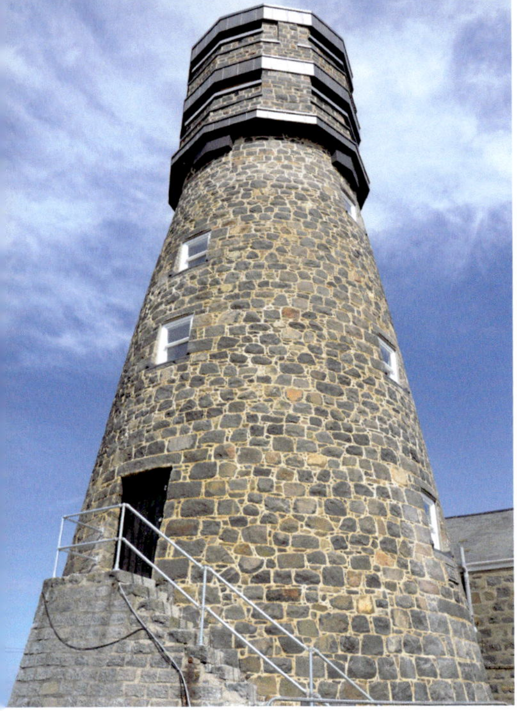

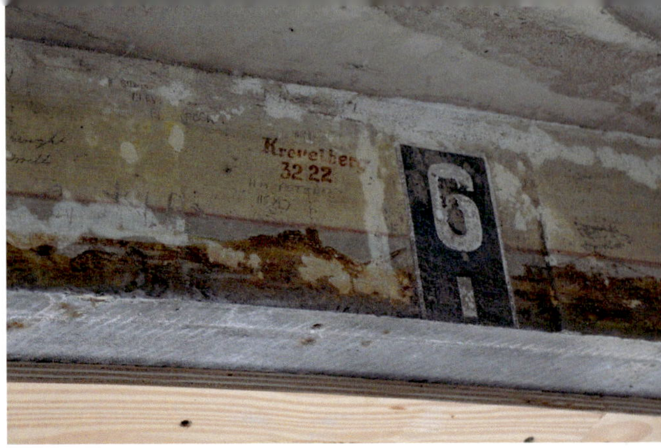

Above: German range-finder markings. (Soo Wellfair)

Left: Vale Mill. (Soo Wellfair)

the modifications. Ammunition was stored in the very bottom of the mill and the floor was reinforced with concrete, presumably to offer some protection from explosion. They also closed off the bottom doorway and built a stone staircase up the side of the mill which still remains and still acts as the main access point to the mill. The very top floor was removed after the Second World War, mostly due to water damage because of the inefficient dummy ogee cap, but is otherwise structurally quite similar to how it was in the 1940s.

Vale Mill sits right on the edge of a former stone quarry, which was operational until the 1890s when it was taken over by the water board for water storage. The quarry and Vale Mill were both purchased several years ago, as part of an ambitious building development which plans to transform the mill and quarry into a luxurious home.

24. Vale Power Station

In 1903 plans were approved to build a second power station to support the island's first power station located in St Peter Port which had been operational since 1900. The increase in public usage of electricity as well as a booming quarrying industry meant demand could no longer be met. The two sites initially ran alongside one another, with a cable linking the two. Excess power was stored in batteries, which meant the generators did not need to run continuously. The town site closed down in the 1930s and other than a small power station which was installed to run off anthracite and coal during the occupation, the Vale power station has been the only power station in Guernsey since. Most of the island's energy, however, now comes via undersea cables, which link Guernsey, Jersey and France. The power

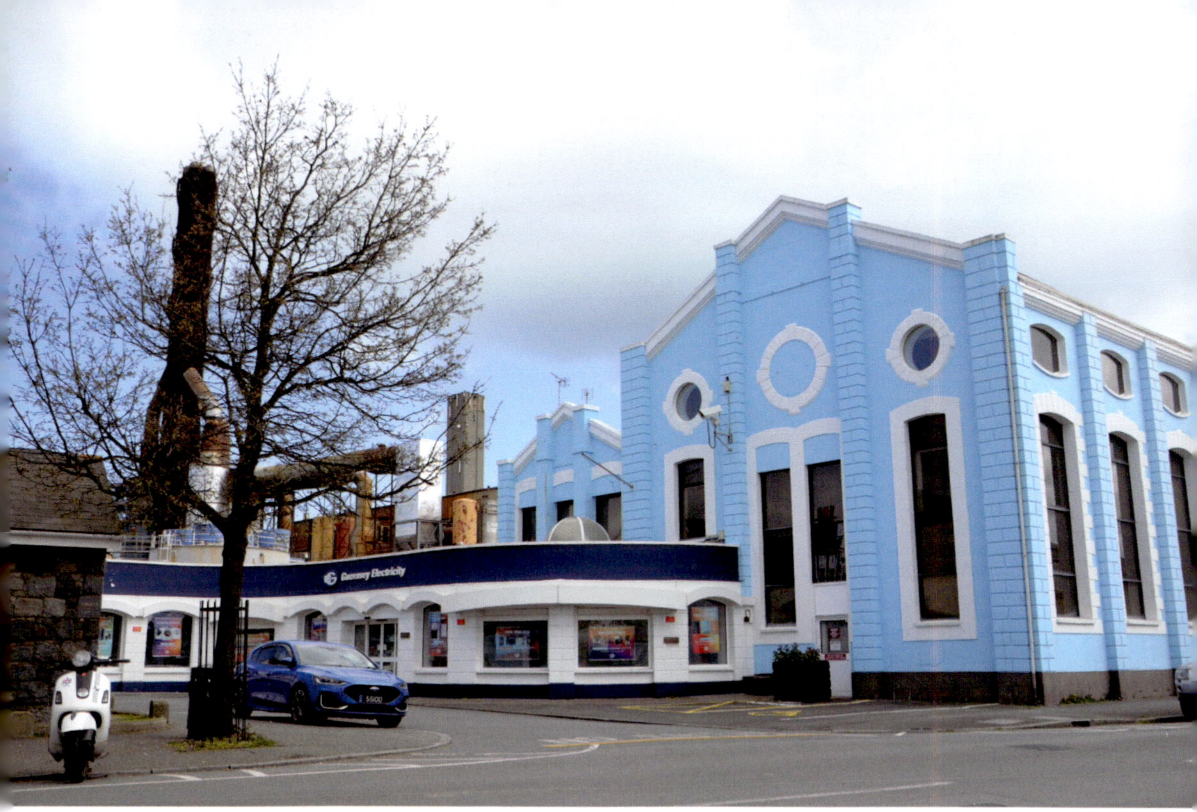

Above: Vale power station and Guernsey Electricity. (Soo Wellfair)

Below: Power station. (Soo Wellfair)

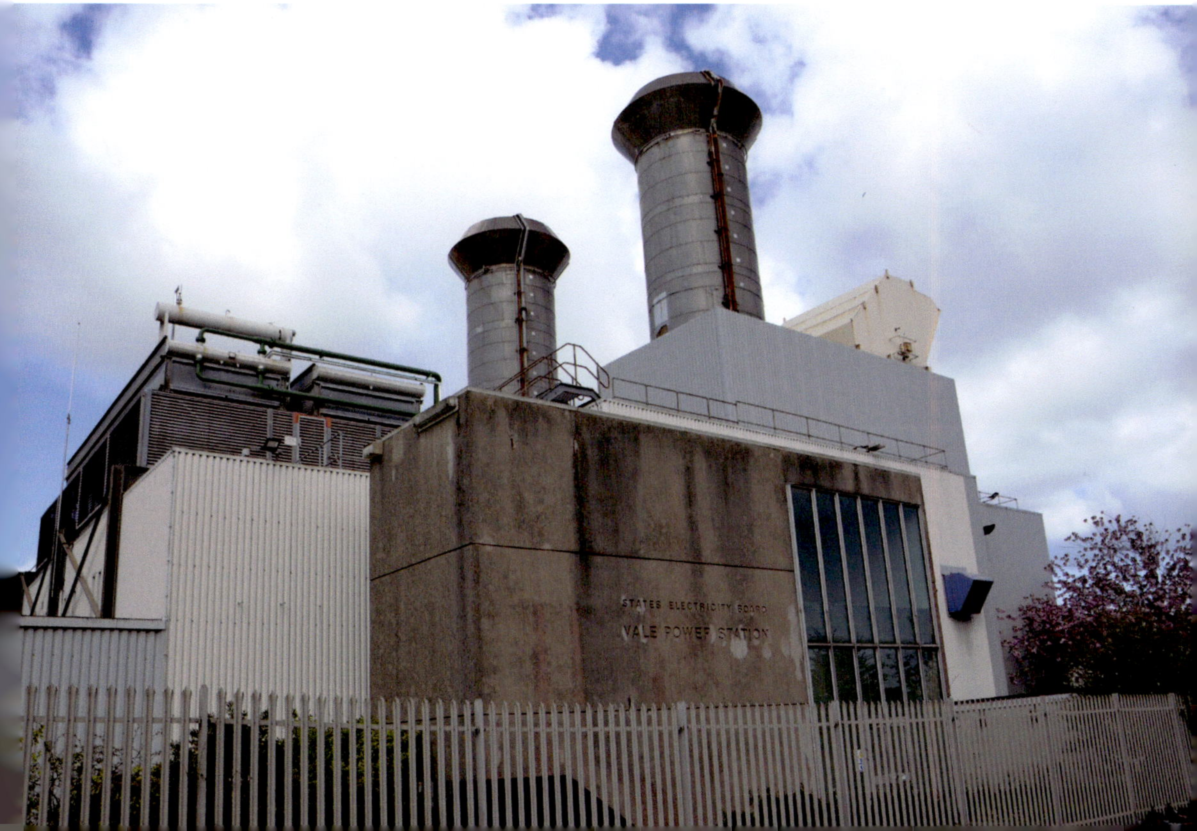

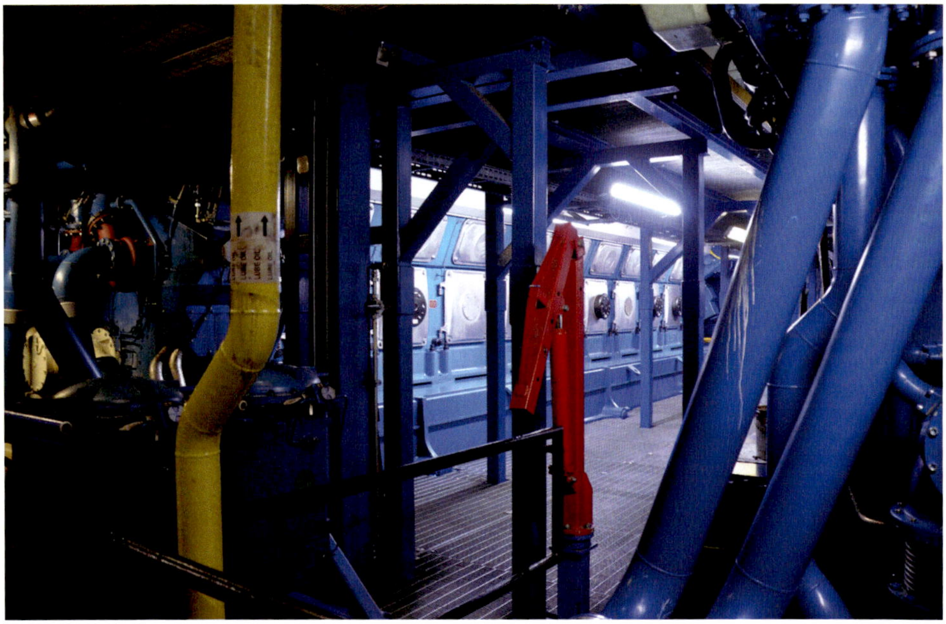

Inside the power station. (Soo Wellfair)

station is still needed to generate its own energy to be able to act as a back-up source but to also provide extra energy during times when consumption is high. The site has expanded much over the years. In the 1960s Hall B was added, in the 1970s Hall C, and finally in the 1980s they added Hall D. In 2014 a 360-tonne engine was installed and made quite a stir in the local press as it was the heaviest piece of machinery to ever have been shipped to Guernsey.

The power station has two quite iconic chimney stacks, particularly the tower located in Hall C, which is known by staff as Thunderbird Three due to its similarity to the TV spacecraft. Standing at 57 metres high, it is the tallest structure in Guernsey.

The Vale Power Station sits alongside St Sampson's harbour, almost on the boundary of the two parishes. It is an easy building to spot. As well as the obvious towers and storage tanks, the original station building, which is located at the very front of the site, has been painted a vivid sky blue. This imposing Edwardian structure is now used as offices and forms part of the Guernsey Electricity retail shop

25. Quarrying Buildings of Northside and Southside

The leading industry in nineteenth-century Guernsey was undoubtedly the quarrying business. With over 250 quarries in use at the peak of the quarrying boom, vast amounts of Guernsey granite were exported off island for use in road building and for more decorative projects such as the steps at St Paul's Cathedral in London. It's thought that over 4 million tons of granite was exported in an industry that was prospering until the late 1960s. There is now just one working quarry in Guernsey, producing stone for local stonemasons and building firms. There is still much evidence of the former quarrying industry, particularly in St Sampson, where the key players in the business, based themselves. This busy port was the perfect location for quarry owner John Mowlem to base his company. Mowlem owned up to 70 per cent of Guernsey's quarries and was certainly the biggest name in the quarrying world at the time, along with his business partners George Burt and Joseph Freeman. The various quarrying sites and associated buildings would have been used as a way to show off the beauty of the stone and the skills of the local stonemasons, so it's not unusual to see quite grand displays of stonework in these ordinarily industrial areas. Many of the buildings standing

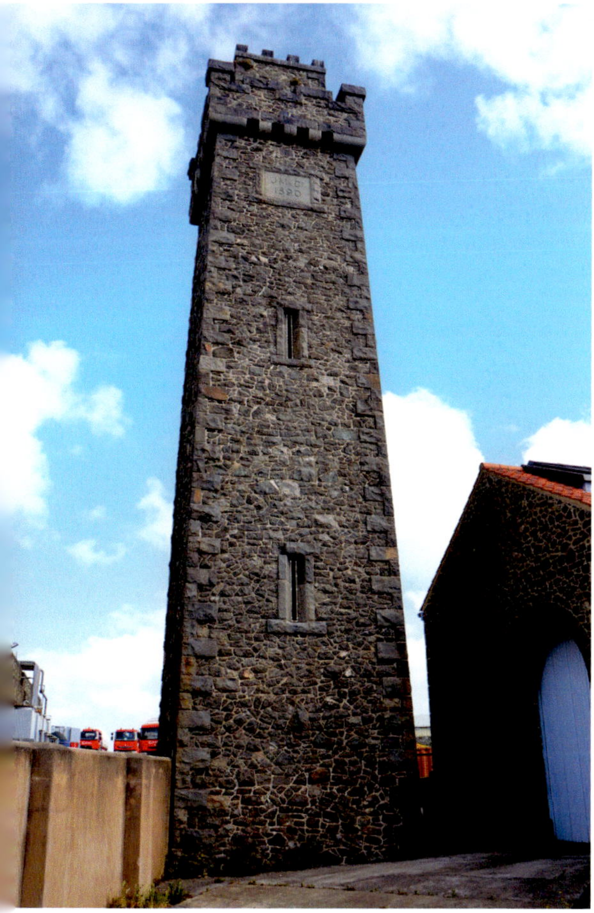

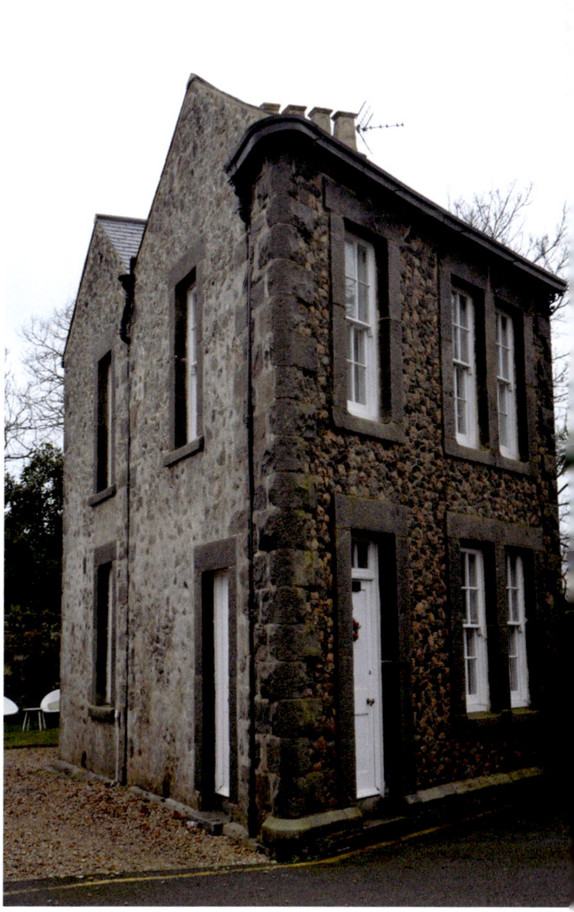

Above left: Mowlem's stone crusher. (Soo Wellfair)

Above right: The NT Triangle House. (Soo Wellfair)

in the Northside and Southside of St Sampson are former quarrying buildings and some still bear the markings of that time, as stonemasons often carved the initials of the quarry owners, as well as their own, into the granite. In just a small area of Northside you will find what was once Mowlem's main office buildings, the blacksmith building which was built solely for the re-shoeing of quarry horses, the grand home of the former quarry manager and the weighbridge building which was used to weigh granite loads before shipping. There is also an impressive tower, styled on the Victoria Tower in St Peter Port, which once housed Mowlem's steam powered stone crusher. Over the other side of the harbour to Southside, next to the parish church, you will find an incredibly quirky little building. Church House is a peculiar little triangular shaped building, which was also once part of John Mowlem's quarrying empire. It was recently renovated by the National Trust of Guernsey and converted into a small home which is now occupied. There are however plans to open part of the site as a tourist attraction, offering an insight into Guernsey's quarrying industry.

26. St Sampson's Church

St Sampson's is thought to be the oldest church in Guernsey. It is dedicated to St Sampson of Dol, the patron saint of Guernsey. St Sampson was born into privilege in Wales in the late fifth century and chose a religious path in life, being ordained as a bishop in the sixth century. He travelled widely, establishing Christian chapels and monasteries, and was believed to have introduced the Christian faith to Guernsey. It is thought that when St Sampson arrived on the island, he established a small wooden chapel near to where the current church stands. It is very difficult to date the church due to a lack of records. However, it is agreed that a church on this site was consecrated in 1111 and there are certainly some remainders of this twelfth-century structure, as well as evidence of significant modifications in the fourteenth century. Before the development of St Sampson's harbour, the church would have originally stood on the shoreline. Much of the church was constructed using local granite, as well as stone from Caen and Chausey. It has been noted that different types of Guernsey granite were used to build different sections of the church, with some walls appearing to be grey and others appearing to be pink or red, which creates quite a contrasting appearance to the exterior.

On entering St Samson's, six steps lead down into the church and the floor is more than over a metre below the doorway.

Many have noticed how the clock in the church is numbered oddly. The numbers are in the format of Roman numerals, yet the number four is shown as 'IIII' and it is believed that this is a reference to the church's date of consecration.

A quite unusual feature of St Sampson's is the saddleback roof which sits atop the church's tower. A saddleback is a type pitched roof with a ridge and two

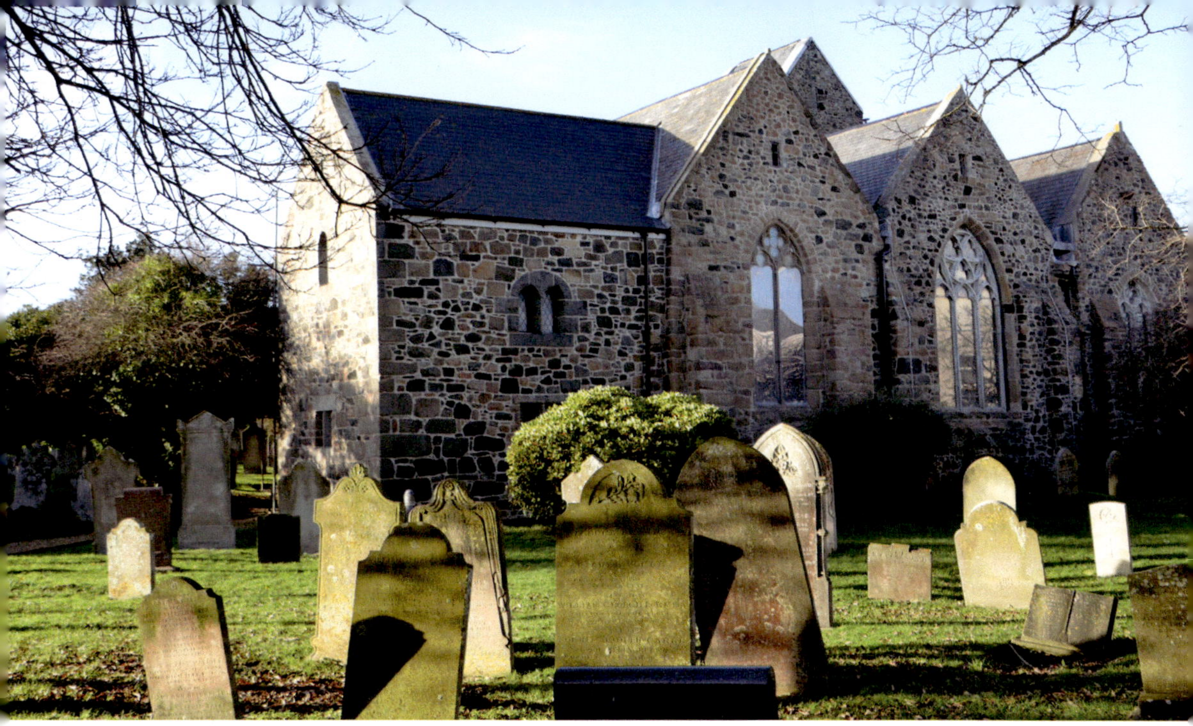

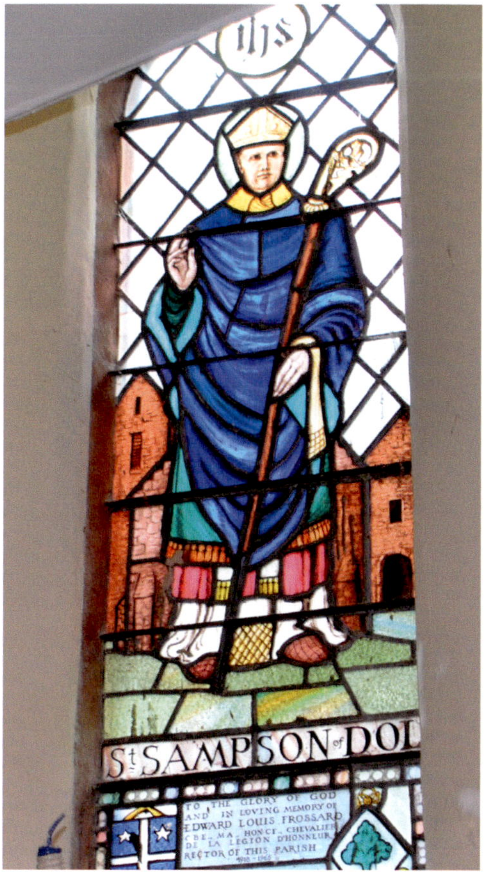

Above: St Sampson's Church. (Soo Wellfair)

Right: Stained-glass window depicting St Sampson. (Soo Wellfair)

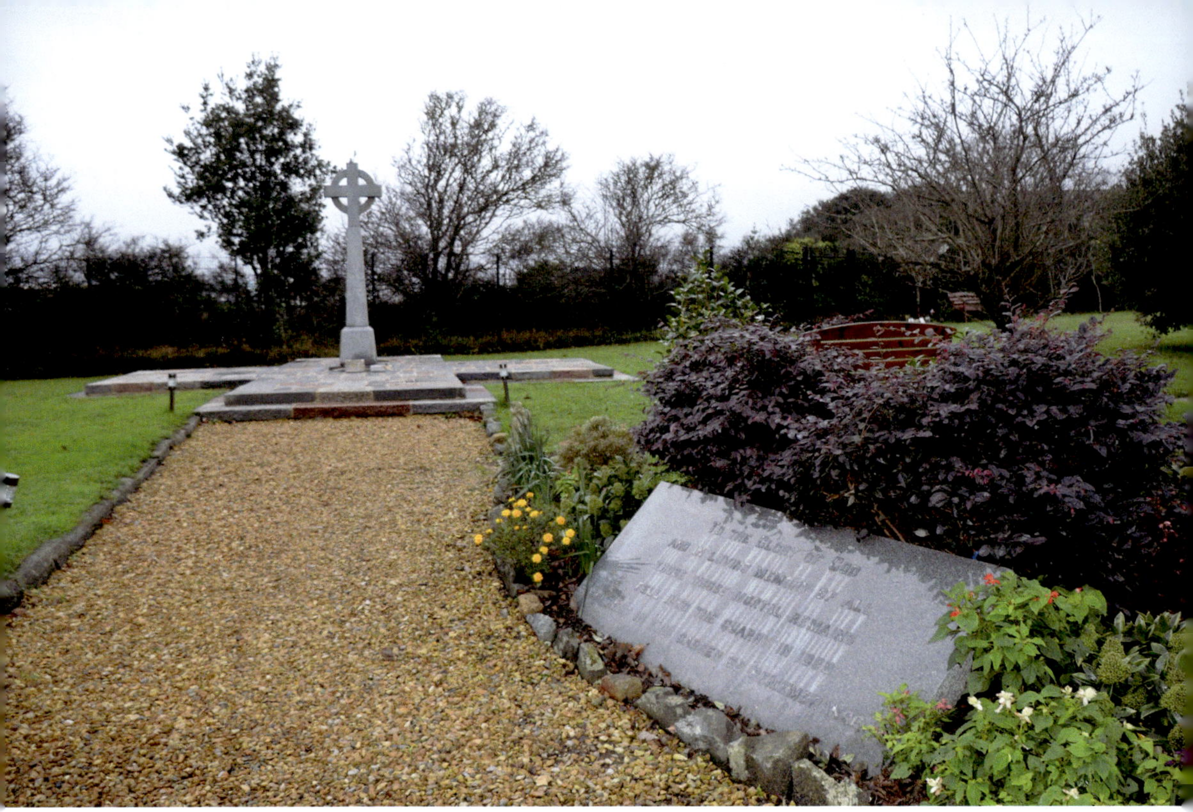

Quarry memorial. (Soo Wellfair)

gables, which is not uncommon for towers in general, but was not a typical design feature on churches.

There is an interesting example of a limestone sundial on the south-west corner of the church. The metal gnomon which casts the shadow on the sundial has been replaced quite recently.

Sadly in 1969, a terrible incident befell St Sampson's Church, when a large section of the churchyard fell into a neighbouring quarry after a shock landslide. Whilst efforts were made to retrieve the graves, many were left as it was just too dangerous to save them. A memorial in the churchyard was put in place to remember those whose graves were lost to the quarry.

27. Oatlands

Oatlands Village is one of Guernsey's most popular visitor attractions, and is tucked away in the north of the island. Although modestly sized, it boasts a variety of retail outlets including amongst others, a pet shop, gift shop, a chocolatier, a craft shop and a goldsmith. It is a picturesque reminder of Guernsey's past with beautiful thatched barns and restored brick kilns, which go back to the days when Oatlands was a brick works. It is thought that a brick works may have been on site from around the late eighteenth century, with the two kilns that are still in situ dating from

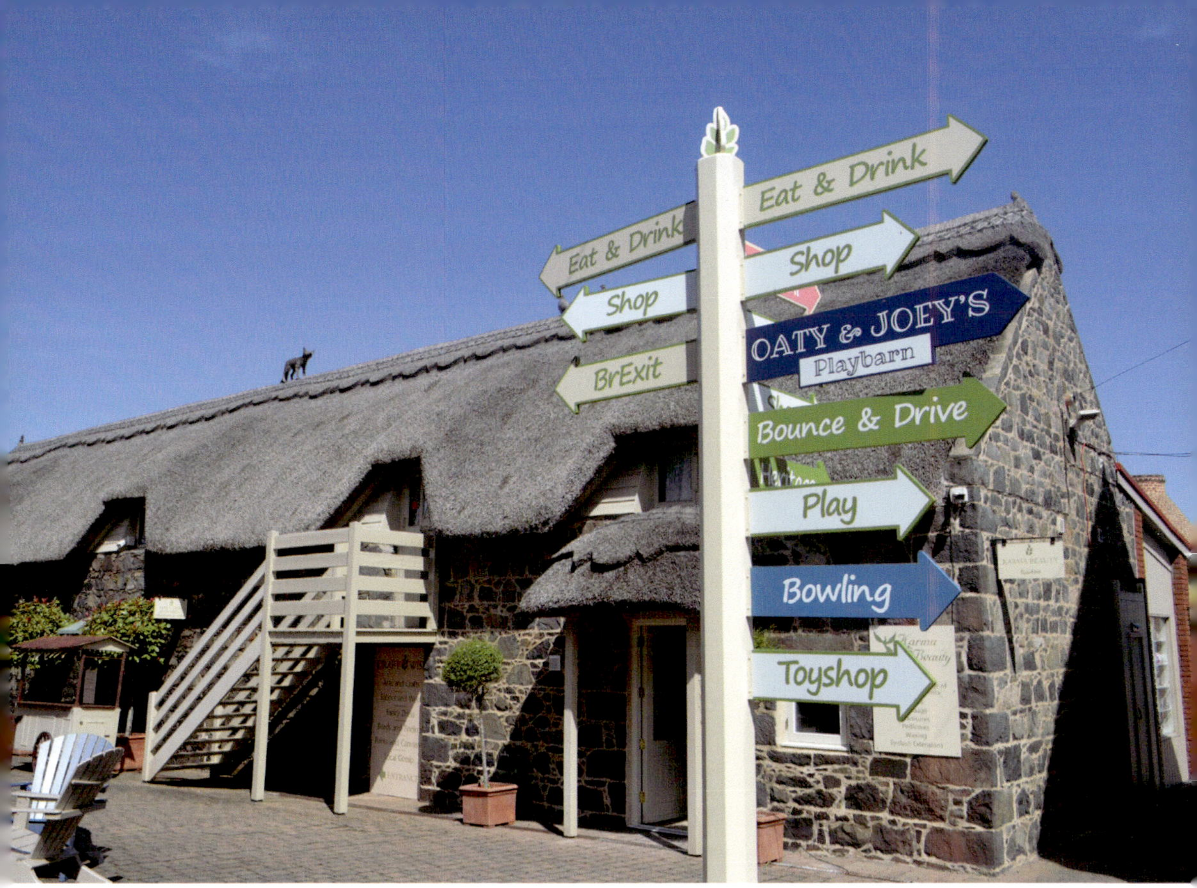

Above: Oatlands. (Soo Wellfair)

Below: Oatlands brick kiln. (Soo Wellfair)

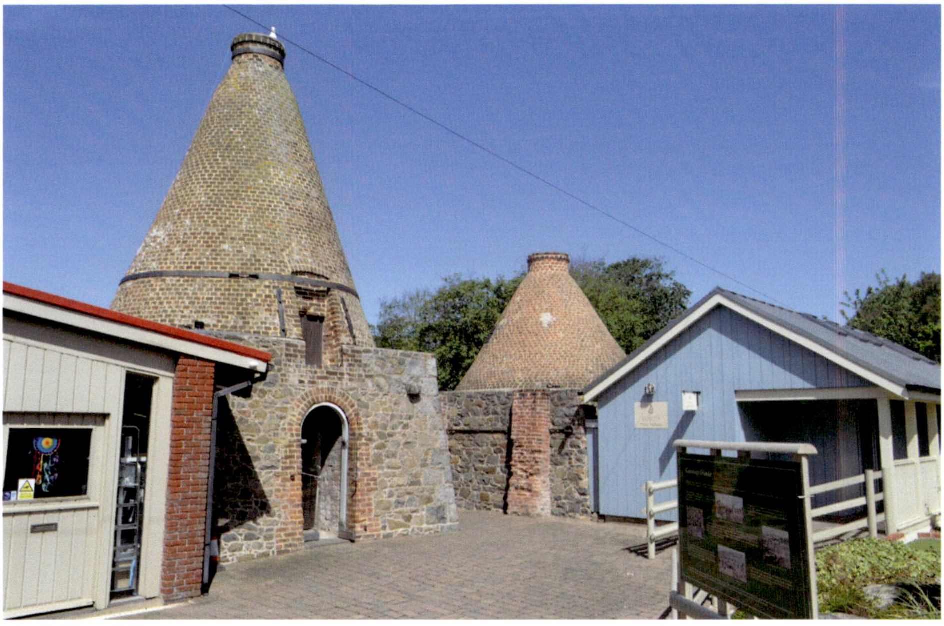

somewhere between 1890 and 1898. As a brick works the site was called La Grande Four, which translates as 'the big oven'. The kilns here were mostly used to fire clay bricks which would have been used in various industries across the island, but most were supplied to the vast numbers of glasshouse sites in operation, with the bricks being used to build chimneys. Although Oatlands is now a retail outlet, it still retains a lot of the original features from its days as La Grand Four. Two large kilns were recently restored and are very much part of the centre's aesthetic. There are information boards scattered around the centre, giving an insight into the industrial past of this once small but busy brickwork. Many of the buildings are original, including the location of the old potter's wheel, which is now a small shop next to the kilns. One of the old kilns has been transformed into a small educational exhibit and both kilns are now registered as ancient monuments. One of the most attractive features at Oatlands are the thatched roofs on the main buildings, complete with ornamental straw animals on the rooftops.

28. Halfway Tram Stop

Now better known as the Halfway bus shelter, this unassuming structure once played an integral part of Guernsey's transportation history. In 1879 Guernsey's first steam tramway was introduced to the island, and upgraded to electric just over a decade later. In fact, it is believed that Guernsey's overhead electric trams were the first of their kind in the British Isles. In 1896, at the halfway point, a small building was erected to serve as a waiting room. Part of the building was set up as a shop and a café, offering refreshments to passengers, and whilst the original building was later replaced by a more modest shelter, these were the beginnings of the Halfway shelter which is still a well-known local landmark today. It even led to the area surrounding it to be known as Halfway, with most people never really knowing the significance of the name. Motor buses were first introduced to help extend the range for the trams in 1909, with Halfway being used as a branch line out to the other side of the island. When the tram service closed down in 1934 the bus routes continued to grow over the decades and the Halfway shelter remained. A little further along the seafront towards St Peter Port, you will also find the former tram depot sheds still standing; now being used by a local coach company. The original tram rails are still very much visible from the roadside. During the Second World War, the occupying forces introduced a road-marking system to make navigating the island for those unfamiliar with the layout and place names. It was a simple system based on colours and numbers, with most routes being marked out with paint on the sides of walls and buildings. Over the years many have faded away completely, yet some have been preserved. In 2013, when the Halfway bus shelter was undergoing some maintenance, one of these German road signs was uncovered and has since been restored and is now quite a feature. It is not the only example of artistry on the building. In 2023 several murals depicting seabirds including the ever-popular puffin, were added.

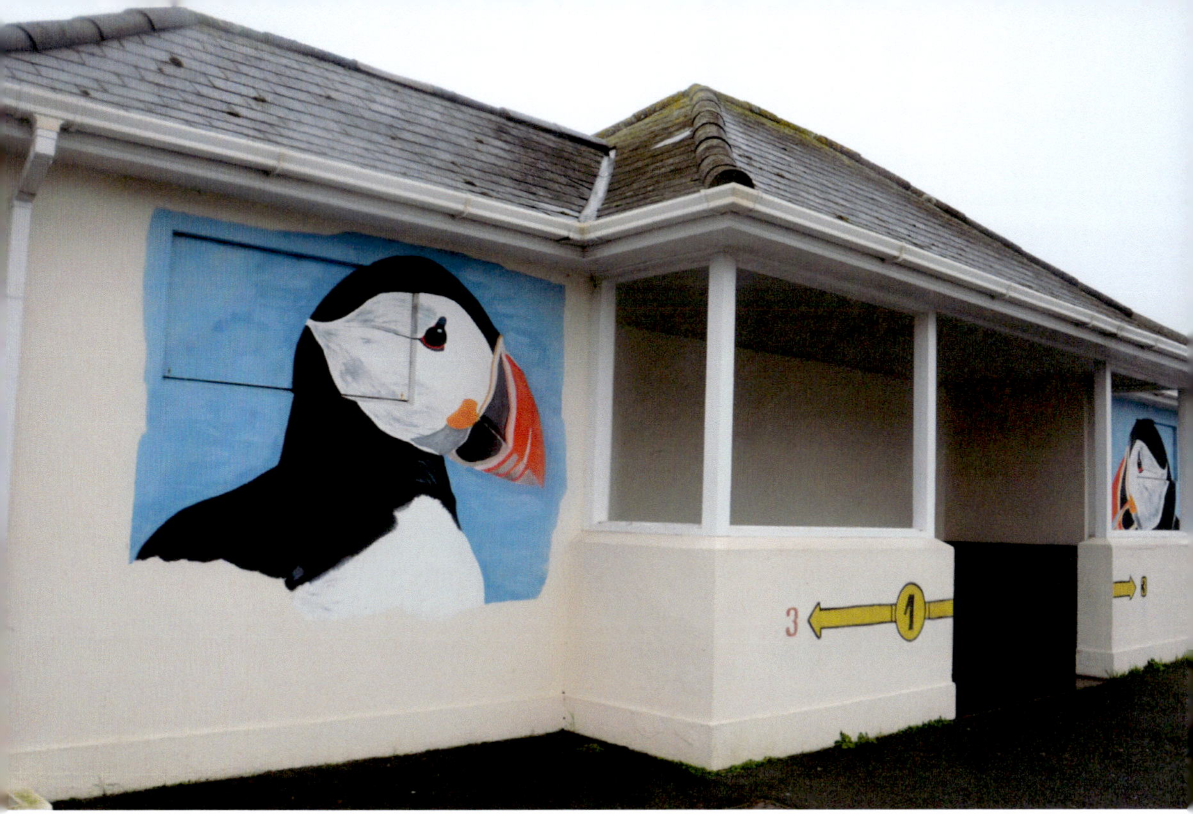

Above: Halfway tram stop with German road marking and murals. (Soo Wellfair)

Below: Former tram shed with tram tracks visible. (Soo Wellfair)

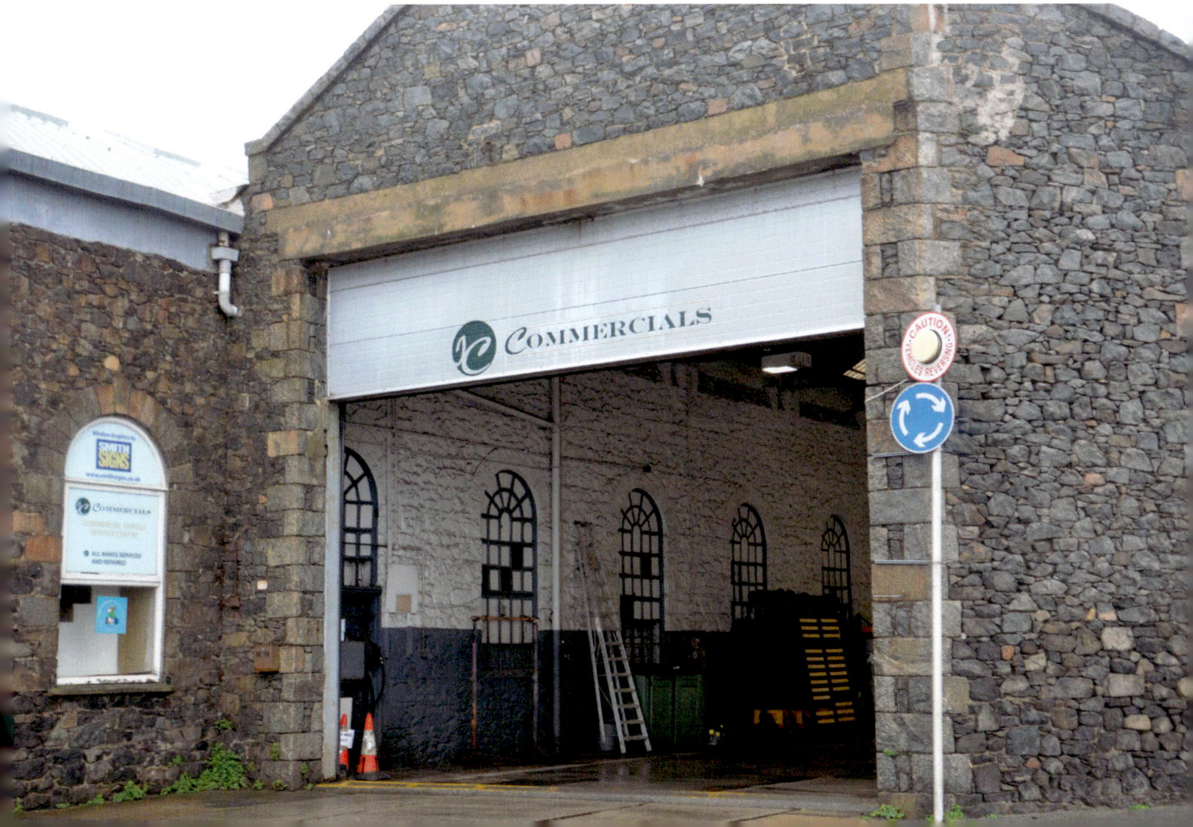

29. St Martin's Church

The parish church of St Martin is formerly known as St Martin de la Bellouse, meaning 'St Martin of the Sloe-Bushes'. It is tucked away behind the main shopping area of St Martin, surrounded by pretty little cottages. The church was probably originally made of wood in the early eleventh century, with a stone structure eventually replacing it completely. It is thought that the oldest part of the church dates back to the thirteenth century, with additions made in the thirteenth and fourteenth centuries and the aisle was completely replaced in the eighteenth century.

The church is named after Martin of Tours or sometimes known as Martin the Merciful. Inside the church you will find the font, which many claim to be the only example of a pre-Reformation font in Guernsey. The pulpit with its Jacobean carvings dates from 1657 and is a beautiful example of this seventeenth-century woodwork. A quirky addition to the church's interior decor is a clarinet displayed in a small cabinet on the wall. This clarinet was used in services to accompany the choir before the first organ was installed in 1848.

St Martin's Church. (Soo Wellfair)

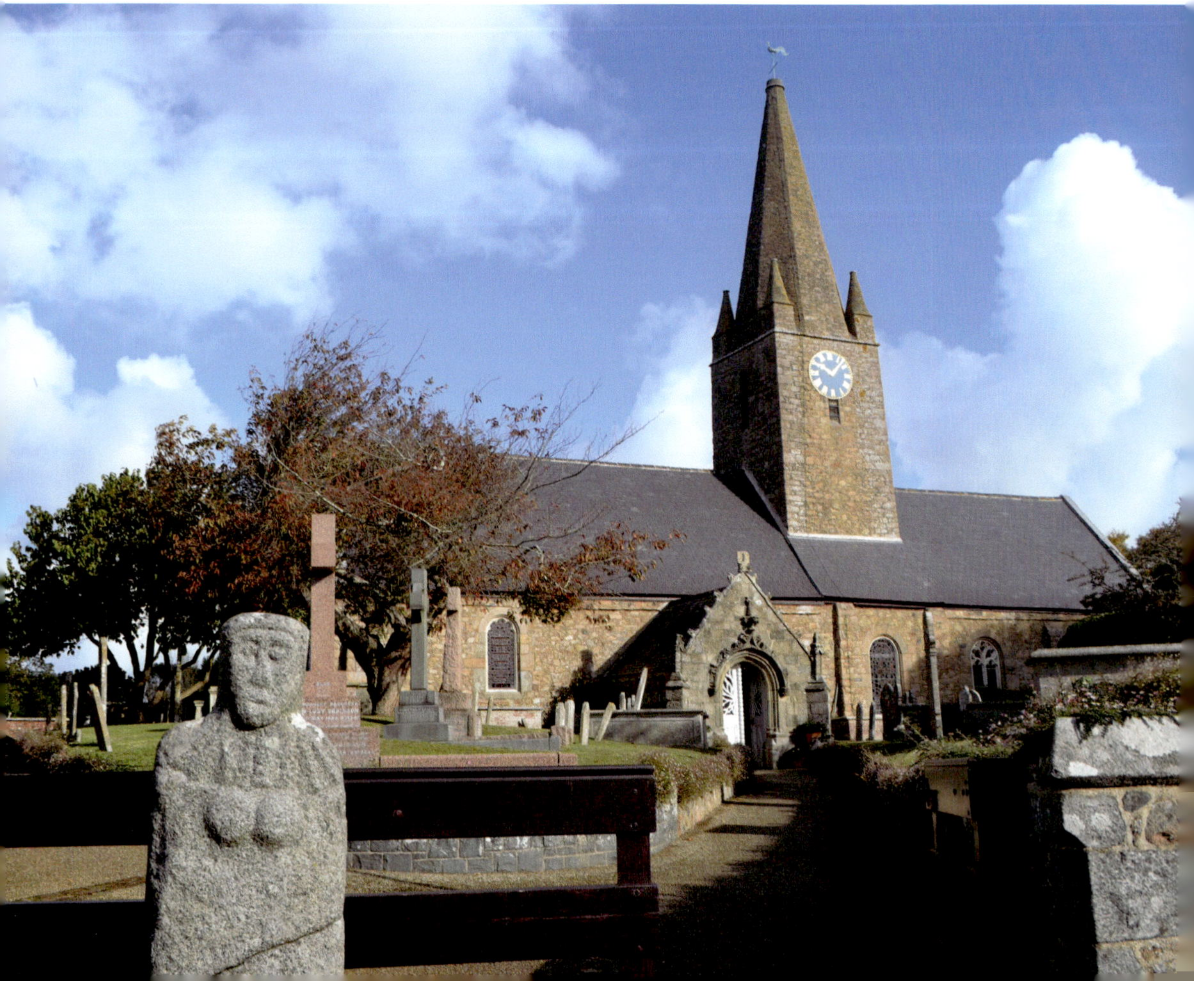

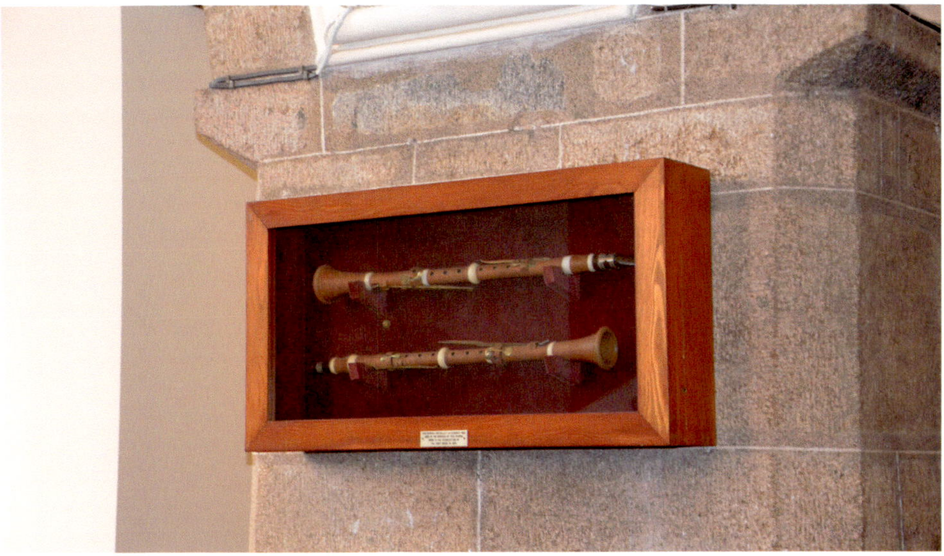

The church clarinet. (Soo Wellfair)

The south porch is a lovely example of the Decorated or the Decorated Gothic style. As well as being quite attractive, it once served an important parochial function. The two long benches set with the porch were once where the local Douzaine or parish council would meet for their meetings.

Probably the most well-known feature of St Martin's Church is La Gran'mère du Chimquière, an impressive stone menhir, standing outside the church gates. The Grandmother of the Cemetery is a very old lady indeed and this stone carving is thought to have originally been created around 4,000 years ago and re-carved about 2,000 years ago. Nobody knows exactly where she came from or why she was created, although from the twentieth century onwards she has been seen as an earth goddess and a fertility symbol. It is traditional for brides getting married at the church to adorn the statue with flower garlands and coins for good luck. It is thought that La Gran'mère was previously located within the grounds of the churchyard and was moved outside the gates by a clergyman who disapproved of her pagan roots. This could also explain how she came to be broken in half.

30. Sausmarez Manor

Sausmarez Manor is a stunning manor house located in the parish of St Martin. It is possible that parts of the house may date back to as early as the twelfth century, although very little of that original building exists today. The house has been extended and modified on many occasions and as a result has parts which also date back to the Tudor, Queen Anne, Regency and Victorian eras. It would originally have been the manor house of what was known as a fiefdom. Fiefs were part of Guernsey's old Norman feudal system which determined land ownership and division, and each one belonged to a Seigneur, who was effectively the lord of the manor.

The most iconic view of Sausmarez Manor today is the beautiful front of the house, which was built in the popular Queen Anne Colonial style in the early eighteenth century. The Widow's Walk is an interesting feature, likely inspired by similar examples in North America. An impressive set of iron gates at the entrance to the property, bears the de Sausmarez family crest and also features statues of a unicorn and a greyhound, sculpted by well-known eighteenth-century monumental mason, Sir Henry Cheere.

Sausmarez Manor. (Soo Wellfair)

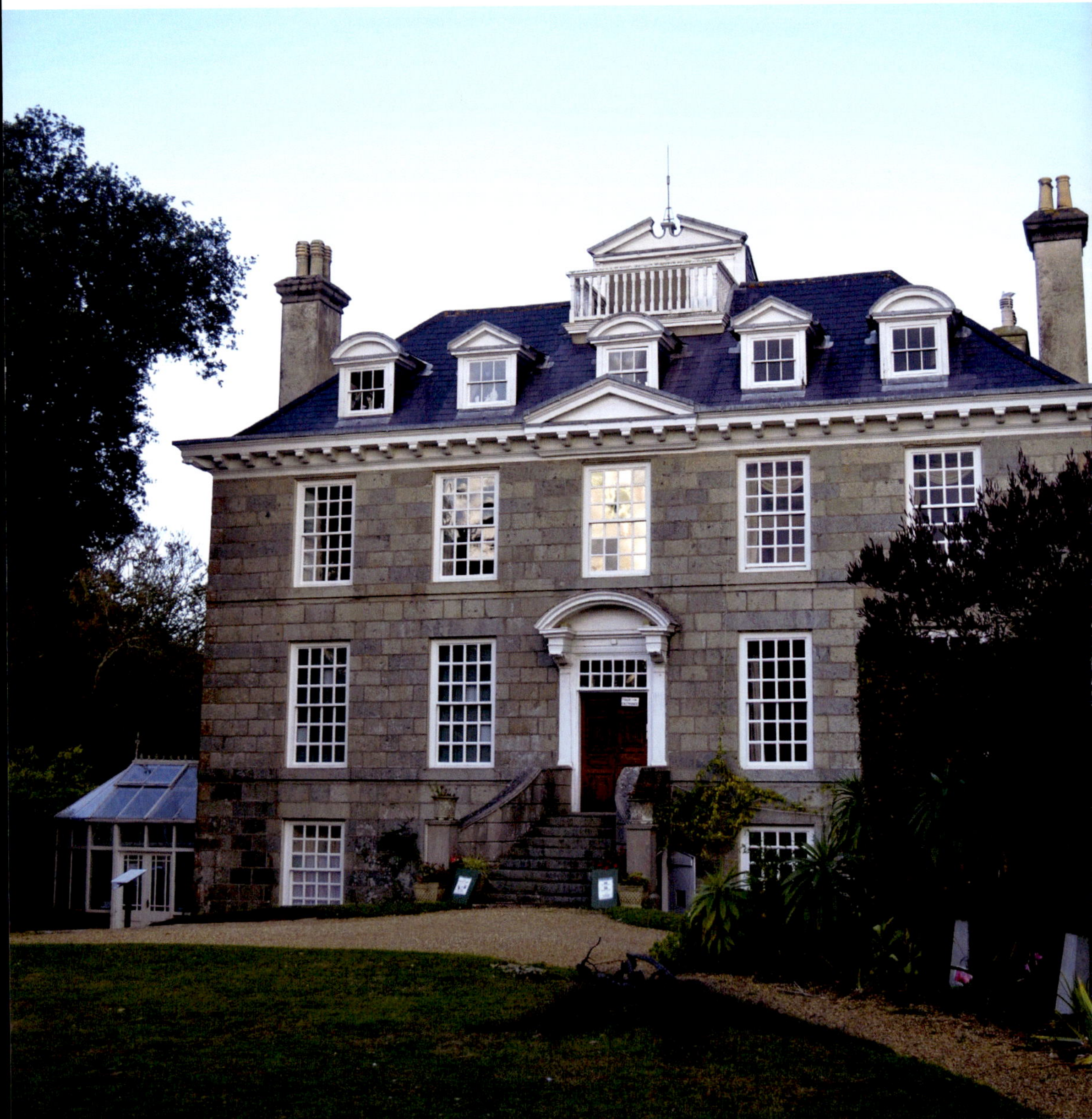

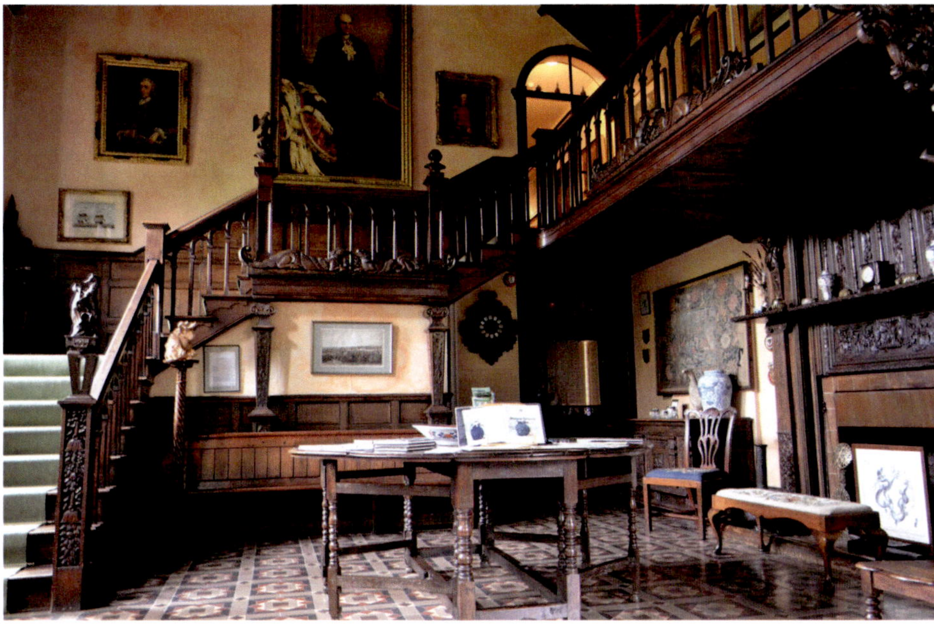

Sausmarez Manor hallway. (Soo Wellfair)

During the occupation (1940–45) many large homes in Guernsey were taken over by the occupying forces. Sausmarez Manor would have been quite an attractive requisition, although it was never taken. The reason being the occupant at the time, Sir Havilland de Sausmarez, had refused to install electric lighting in the property!

The house and grounds are open to the public, with guided house tours on offer throughout the year. Visitors can also enjoy the subtropical gardens, sculpture trail, train rides, a pitch and putt course, a coppersmiths, a gift shop and café. During the warmer months a busy farmers' market is held in the grounds every Saturday morning.

31. Victor Hugo's Haunted House and Mount Herault

As a result of the American War of Independence (1775–83), followed by the French Revolutionary Wars (1792–1802) and Napoleonic Wars (1803–15), Guernsey became extremely vulnerable to French attack for quite an extended period. It was because of these uncertain times that it was decided to improve the island's defences with a number of towers, gun batteries and watch-houses, which were positioned around the coast.

The watchtowers were constructed as part of a signalling system, employed to send warnings via a chain of beacons along the coastline, to one of the main military posts such as Fort George in St Peter Port. These were manned by the Royal Guernsey Militia, who kept watch overnight from 5 p.m. to 7 a.m. every day.

Mont Herault is one of the better known of the old watchtowers and whilst it is not possible to go inside, visitors can go to the site which is located in the elevated south-west of Guernsey. It is well preserved with an information board in situ. The watchtowers were all constructed using local granite and were designed with a sloped, slate roof. Mont Herault would have been designed as a one-storey unit with two ground-floor rooms, separated by a corridor. This would have been the main living area for those on duty, with the loft space above being mostly used for storage. However, it is believed that soldiers may have slept in the loft in colder months to keep warm.

Just a little further along the coastline at Pleinmont is another watchtower. This one differs for several reasons. Firstly, it was the only watchtower to have been built with two storeys, so it looked slightly different in design to the other watch houses, which all looked quite uniform.

Known officially as the Pleinmont Tower, the watchtower was later known by most as 'Victor Hugo's Haunted House'. This is because the building was referenced in his 1866 novel *Toilers of the Sea*. Hugo describes the house as being in a very 'lonely spot' and notes that the windows resemble empty eye sockets. Sketches that Hugo made of the house certainly capture the bleakness and eeriness of the old watch-house and helped the building gain its reputation of being haunted. In the early twentieth century, the sloped roof was replaced with a flat one and Pleinmont watch-house continued to be used as a signalling and

Mont Herault watch house. (Soo Wellfair)

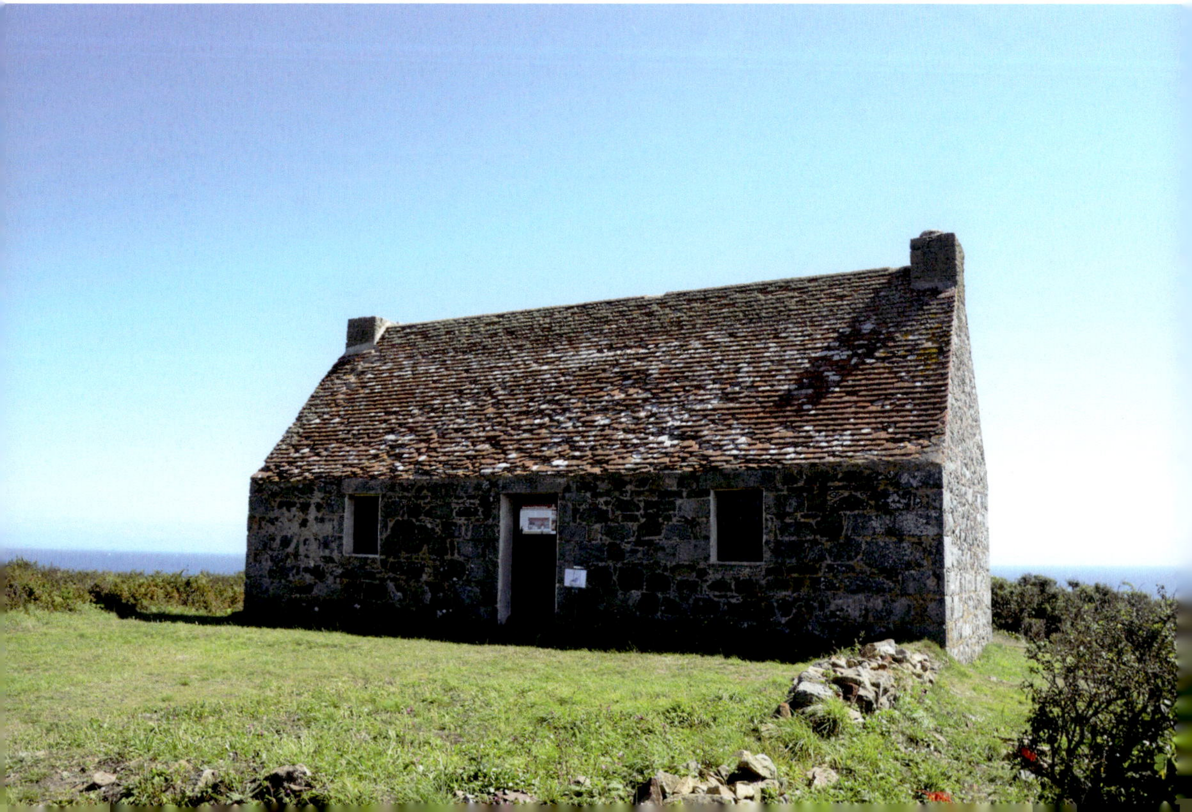

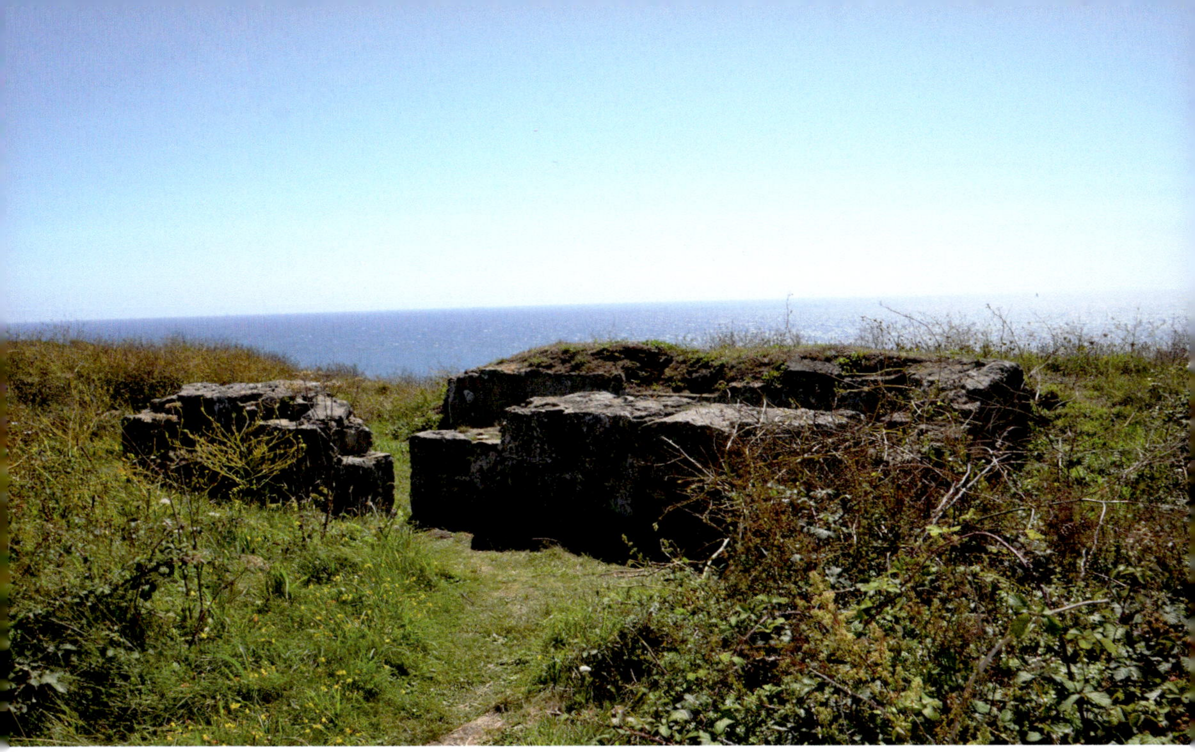

Above: Remains of Victor Hugo's 'haunted house'. (Soo Wellfair)

Below: Lintel from Pleinmont watch house, Guernsey Museum. (Soo Wellfair)

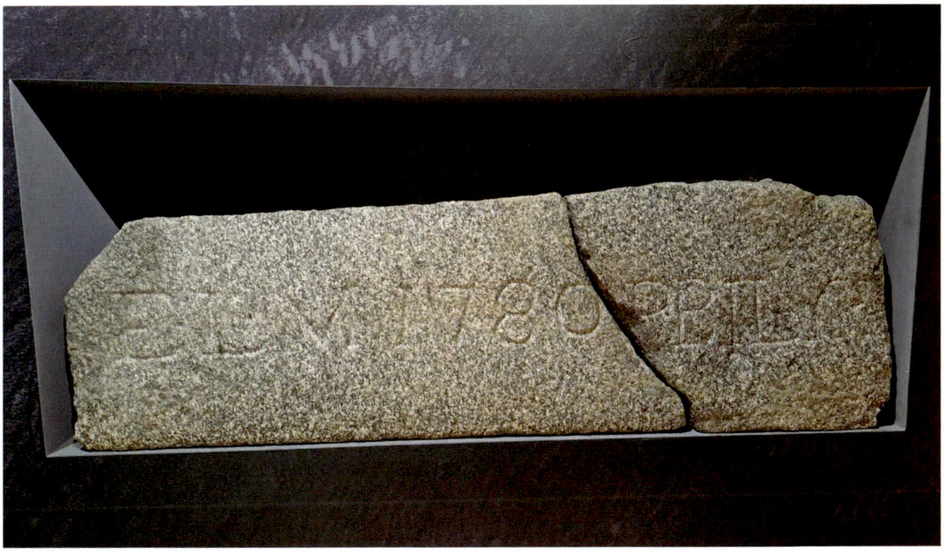

semaphore station long after its counterparts. It eventually became a tearoom for some time before being destroyed during the occupation, as it stood in the firing line of a very large gun placement which had been installed in the area. The ruins are still visible and despite there being very little left of the structure, it is still a popular attraction for Victor Hugo fans.

32. Forest Church

Forest parish church, known officially as St Marguerite de la Forêt, is the highest church in Guernsey. The Forest parish is situated in the south of the island, where some areas have an altitude of around 100 metres. As well as being the highest church in Guernsey, it is also the smallest. The church as it currently stands has parts dating from as early as the thirteenth century, with later additions added in the fifteenth century. There were significant changes made to the layout in the late nineteenth century, when the floor of the nave was lowered by almost 20 inches. There is, however, evidence to suggest there was an older church or chapel on the site, predating the existing structure by several hundred years. The site itself was also certainly used during the prehistoric times as there are several examples of Neolithic stones in the area, including some which have been incorporated into the walls of the current church.

The church has some beautiful stained-glass windows including one from the nineteenth century, which depicts St Marguerite of Antioch, a martyr and patron saint of pregnancy and childbirth. An odd quirk about the windows in Forest Church is that no two window openings are the same.

In the 1980s the four bells of the church (a pair for the seventeenth century and the other from the nineteenth century) were increased to a ring of six.

The church clock was installed in 1897 to mark Queen Victoria's diamond jubilee. It was installed by the German clockmaker Ernsy W. Bachman, and chimes on the hour, plus every half hour.

Forest Church. (Soo Wellfair)

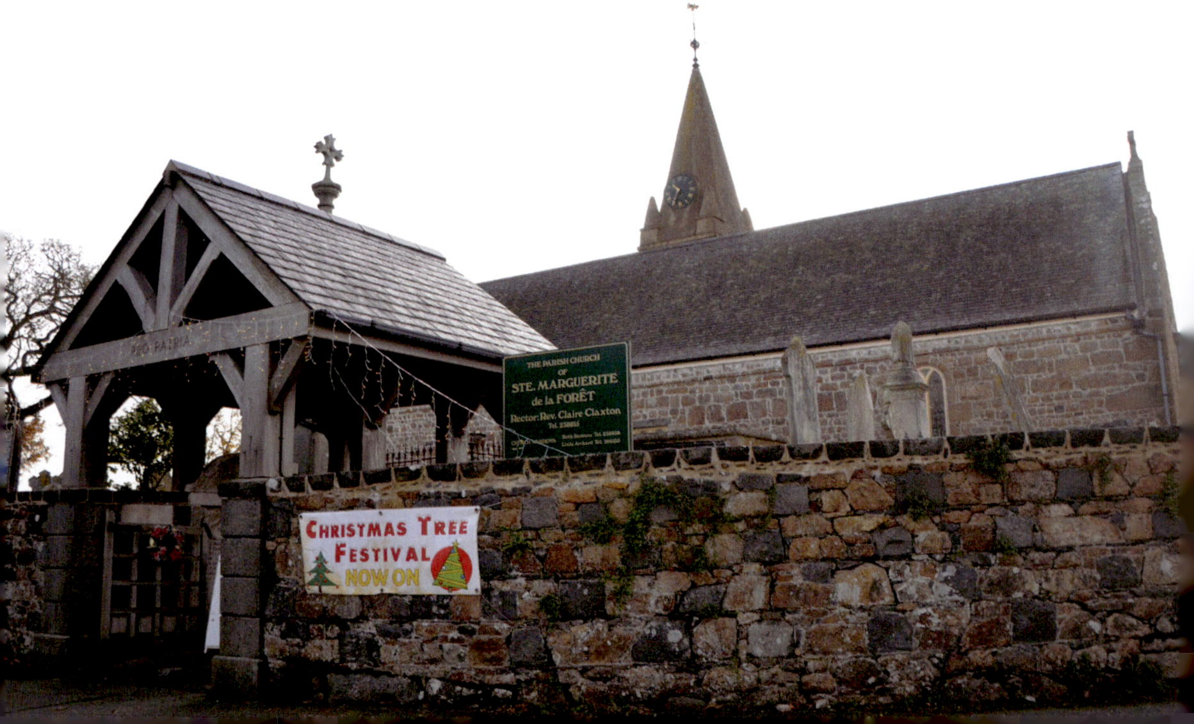

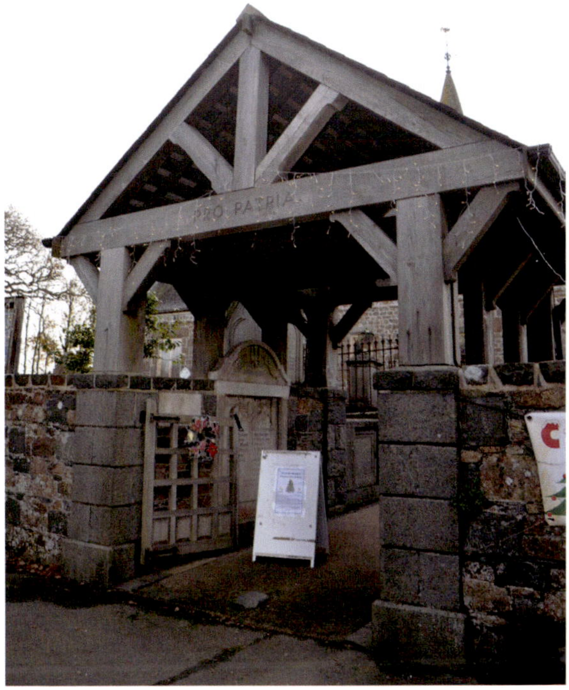

Forest Church war memorial lychgate. (Soo Wellfair)

Whilst the church is built primarily of Guernsey granite, some of the interior was constructed using a much softer stone from the Chausey Islands. Whilst Guernsey was once well known as a quarrying island with many local buildings being made from the local stone, it was considered too hard for carving intricate and ornate designs and stone was often imported for this reason.

The church spire, like many, features an attractive weathervane. The one you will see today, however, is a replacement. The original vane was apparently used for target practice during the Second World War and was removed, later to be installed at the nearby Forest Primary School.

Another attractive feature outside the church is the wooden lych gate, which also serves as a war memorial and was installed in 1952.

33. Guernsey Airport

Guernsey airport can be found in the Forest parish in an area called La Villiaze. It was opened in 1939 after replacing the short-lived and much blighted aerodrome based at L'Eree on the west coast of the island. The new airport was built at a cost of £100,500 and was made up of four grass runways and a main terminal building and started off with scheduled flights to London and Southampton. Approximately 5,000 passengers had travelled through the airport

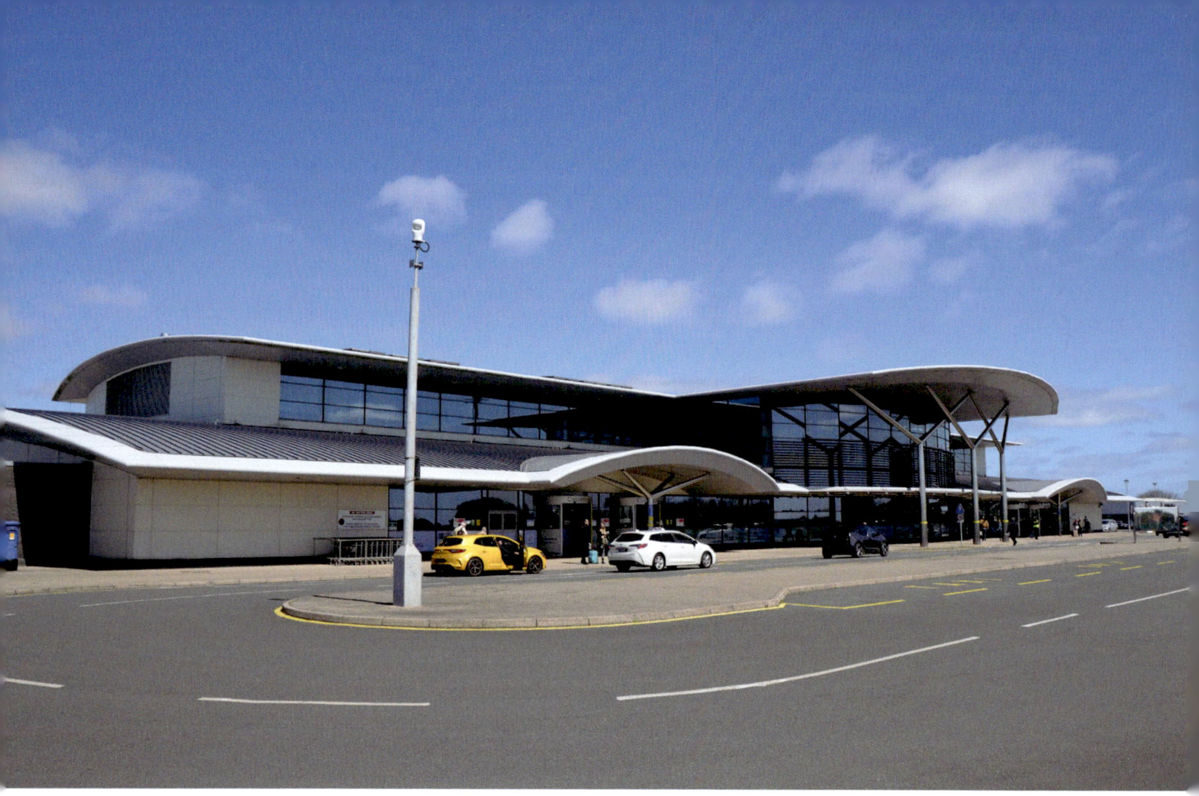

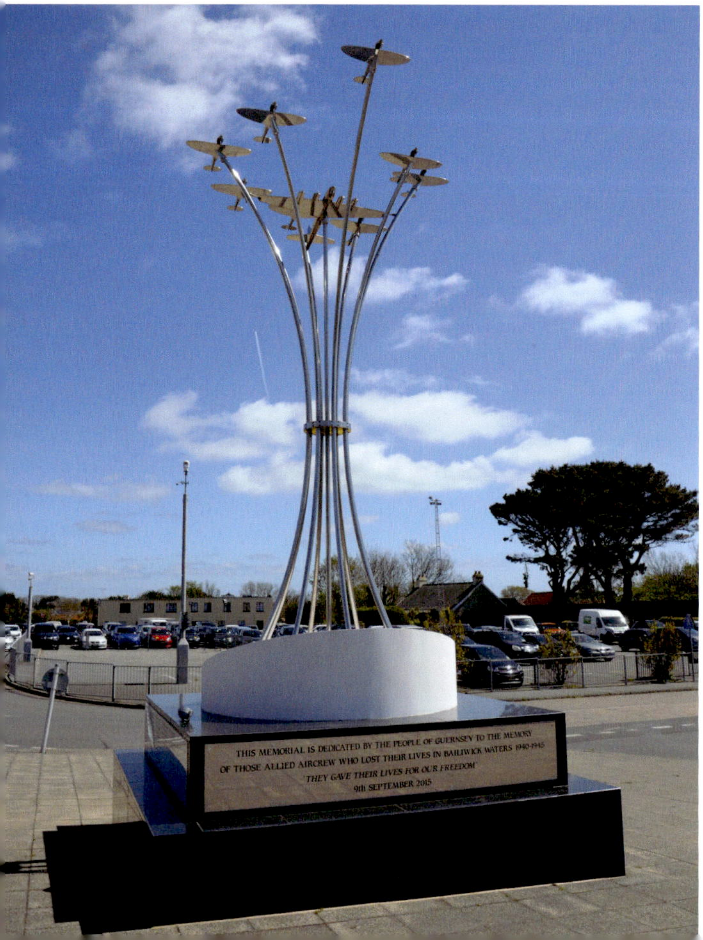

Above: Guernsey airport. (Soo Wellfair)

Left: Allied Aircrew memorial. (Soo Wellfair)

before the occupation of Guernsey during the Second World War, putting a hold on international travel for islanders. The airport was open during the occupation, but was strictly for military use only.

In June 1945, a month after Liberation Day, King George VI and Queen Elizabeth arrived at Guernsey airport on an official post-war visit. Not long after, normal operations resumed and regular scheduled flights were reinstated for the first time properly since the airport had first opened. Over the years, many improvements were made as the aviation and tourism industries grew, including the addition of radar in the 1950s, a new 1,463-metre asphalt runway in 1960, and state-of-the-art landing systems in the 1970s. In 2004 a brand-new terminal opened, followed by an extensive redevelopment of the runway and surrounding areas shortly after.

Guernsey airport currently employs around 650 workers in various positions including a dedicated fire service division of thirty-three firefighters.

In 2015 a war memorial was installed in front of the airport. The Allied Aircrew Memorial is dedicated to the 153 Allied pilots who lost their lives in the Bailiwick of Guernsey between 1940 and 1945. The sculpture depicts seven war planes (a Boeing B17 and six Spitfires). A yearly ceremony takes place in September and features a commemorative flyover and the laying of a wreath.

34. St Peter's Church

St Peter's is the parish church of St Pierre du Bois (St Peter in the Wood). This pretty Anglican church is situated within a small valley and is the focal point of this rural parish. The church standing today is likely to have replaced an older structure. It is notoriously difficult to date the older churches of Guernsey, mostly because of the lack of records. The island was repeatedly attacked by neighbouring France after becoming loyal to the English Crown in the thirteenth century. Most, if not all, of Guernsey's parish churches were ransacked and ruined during these attacks, so it is likely that we can date the majority to the fourteenth or fifteenth century. It is also possible that the church also sits on what was once a Pagan site, and the stream that runs beneath the church from the altar is a solid indicator of this. The church was built without any foundations and is quite well known for having an aisle that slopes significantly from west to east, with a height difference of just under 2 metres. Locals joke that it is the only church known where the couple marrying must walk up the aisle rather than down it!

St Peter's has a set of thirteen seventeenth-century bells, ten of which form the largest bell peal in the Channel Islands.

The church has some interesting features as well as the sloping aisle. A small but beautiful stained-glass window depicts St Peter, the patron saint of fishermen. He is, quite appropriately, wearing a traditional Guernsey jumper, known simply as a guernsey. These hard-wearing woollen jumpers were originally designed for

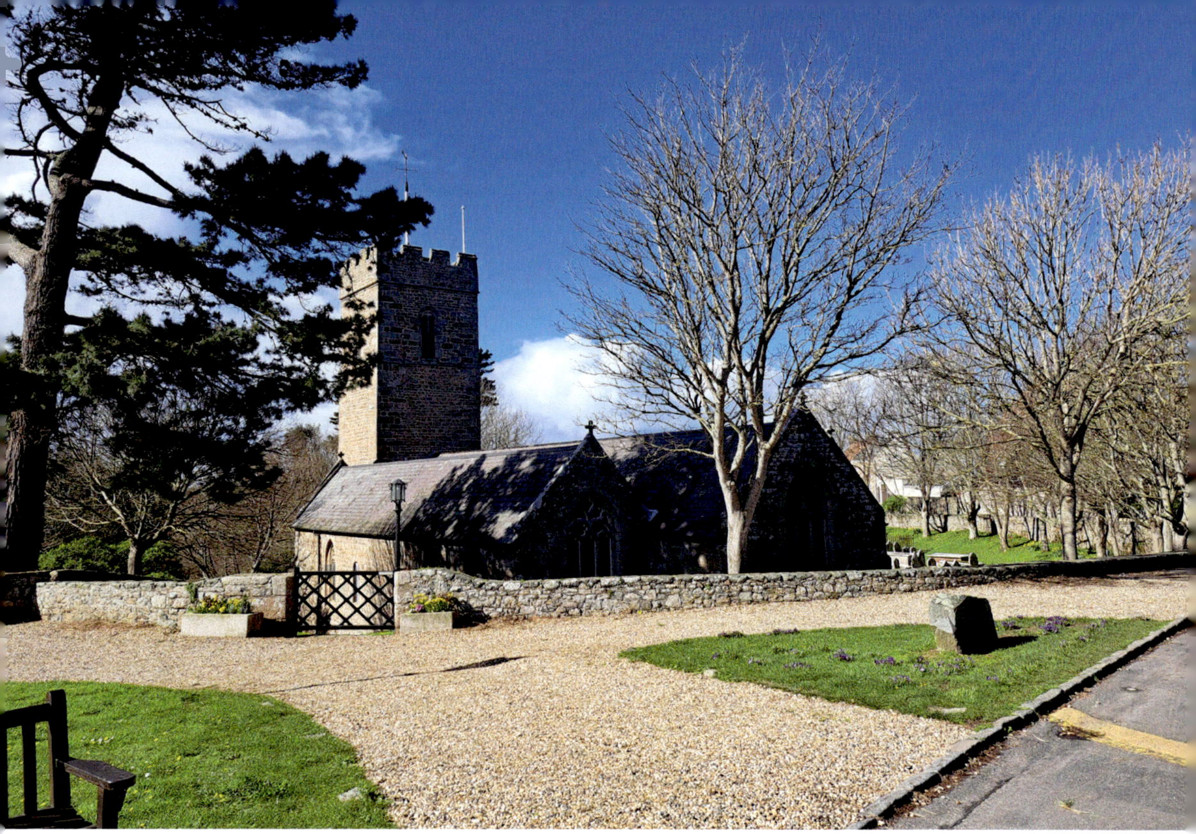

Above: St Peter's Church. (Soo Wellfair)

Below left: The legendary pirate grave. (Soo Wellfair)

Below right: Stained-glass window depicting St Peter wearing a guernsey. (Soo Wellfair)

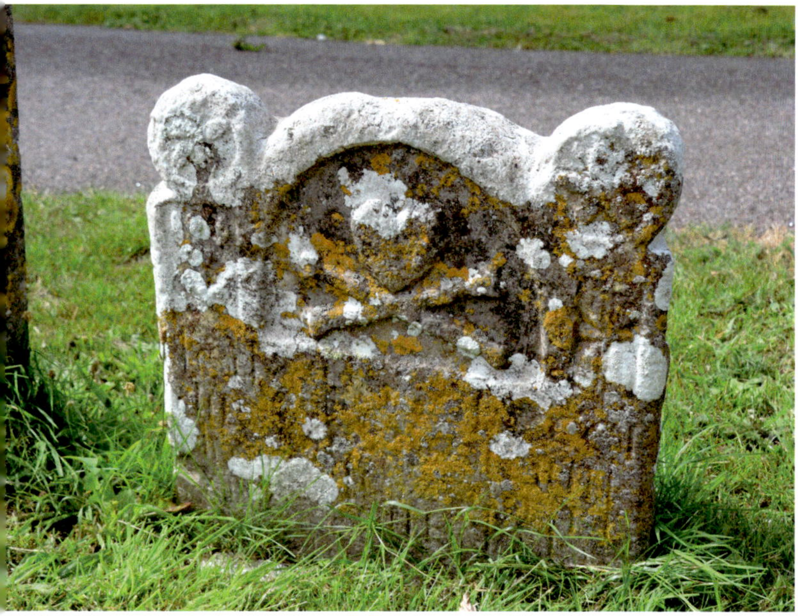

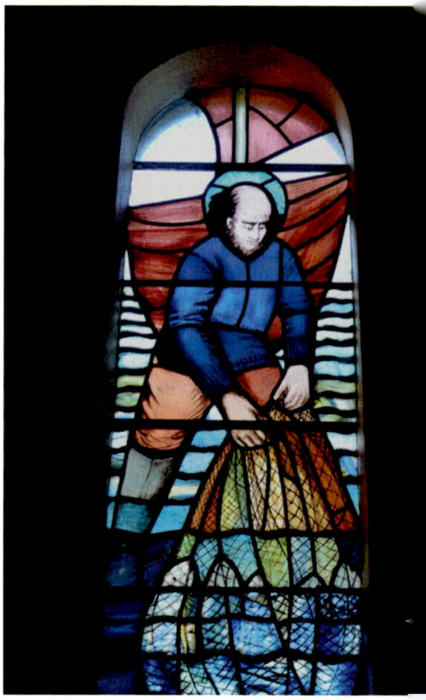

fishermen as they gave protection against the harsh elements and are still very much a part of Guernsey culture today.

Whilst it is thought that the current church was almost certainly built using what was left of the original Norman structure, it is also a possibility that some much older stones were incorporated into the building. There is a 7-foot-long slab built into one of the walls, which juts out significantly. It was clearly placed there quite deliberately which would suggest a prehistoric megalith was chosen for its magical qualities.

A fun feature outside in the churchyard is what some believe to be a genuine pirate grave, with a skull and crossbones marked on the headstone. It sits amongst the many headstones, in a churchyard where at least thirty generations of St Perrais are buried.

35. Torteval Church

The parish church of Torteval, dedicated to St Philip, is one of Guernsey's most distinctive-looking churches. Surprisingly, it is also one of the youngest. Designed by the famous Cumbrian architect John Wilson, Torteval Church was built in 1816 after the original twelfth-century church was condemned after falling into disrepair. The original church came with quite an intriguing backstory. Legend has it Philip de Carteret of Jersey was caught in a terrible storm at sea, and vowed that if he made it safely ashore he would build a church nearby as a way to show his appreciation for being saved. His vessel landed at Rocquaine Bay and true to his word he built the original Torteval Church.

The 'new' church has become something of a local landmark due to its striking appearance. Wilson's design is quite unlike anything else in Guernsey, in particular the now iconic round tower, crenellations and tall spire. Torteval Church has the tallest church spire in Guernsey, so much so that it was once used as an unofficial sea marker. It had been discussed to add a light to the spire and have the church officially registered as a navigational beacon, but Trinity House rejected this idea.

The church has three bells, one of which is believed to be the oldest in the Channel Islands, dating back to 1432. The bell is not the only feature of the church which predates the building. The weathervane on top of the spire dates back to 1774, and when work was taking place to repoint and strengthen the tower and spire back in 2017, it was discovered that the wind vane was being kept upright by a 20p piece which had been wedged in to hold it in place. The wind vane and its cockerel were lovingly restored, blessed by the church and reinstated after the restoration work was completed.

Another interesting feature of the church is the baptismal font, which was actually originally located in St Barnabas' Church in St Peter Port before it was closed down in the 1930s.

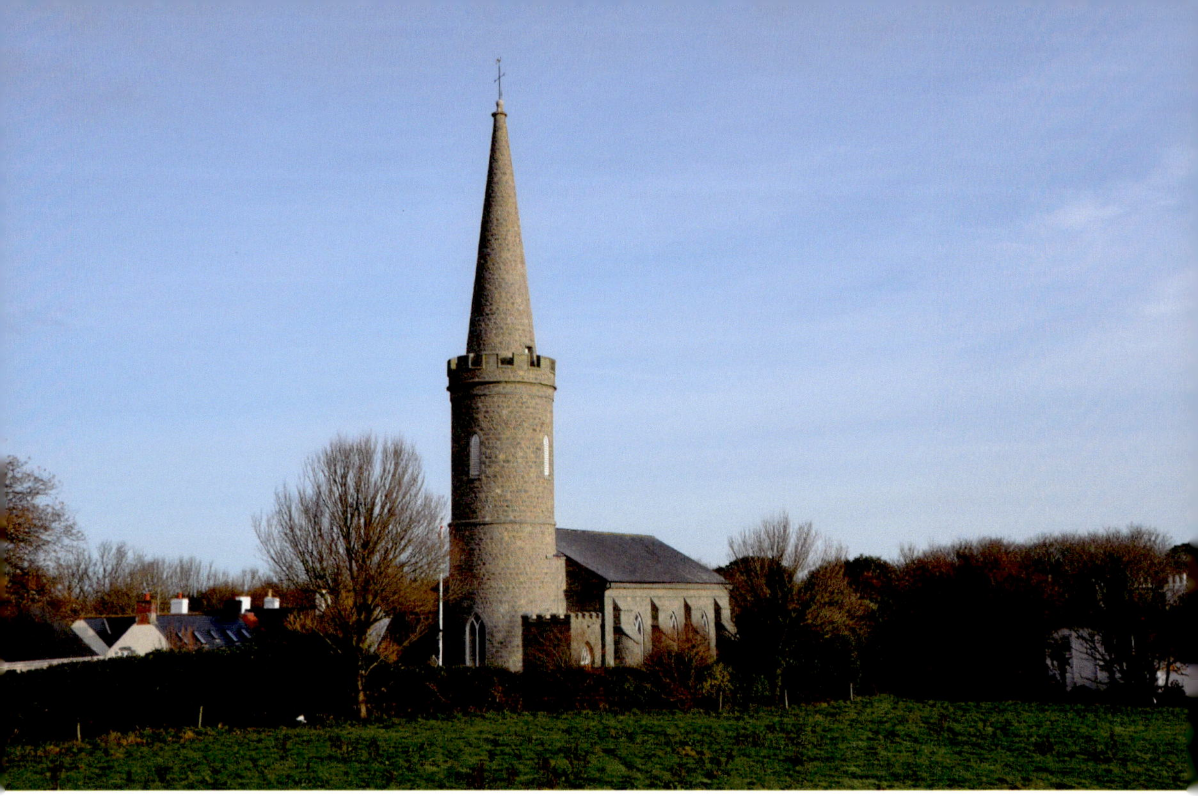

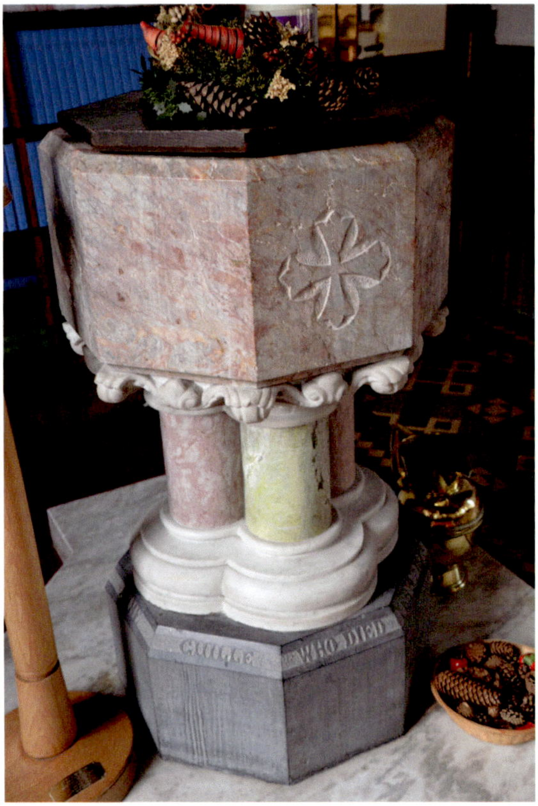

Above: Torteval Church. (Soo Wellfair)

Left: Font, taken from St Barnabas Church. (Soo Wellfair)

Torteval Church is very much the heart of the local community, opening its doors for a wide array of events and occasions throughout the year. Probably the most notable is the Torteval Scarecrow Festival which takes place across two days every summer. The trail of locally made scarecrows and scarecrow montages starts from Torteval Church and makes its way around the quiet parish lanes and attracts around 8,000 visitors each time. It is the church's biggest fundraiser of the year.

36. Hanois Lighthouse

Guernsey's coastal waters are notoriously rocky and hazardous. The huge expanses of rocks, largely hidden at high tide, make navigating the seas around the island very difficult indeed. It is because of this that there have been so many shipwrecks over the centuries, particularly along the west coast and around the south-west tip of the island. Over 120 reported shipwrecks occurred in these areas, which is why islanders campaigned for a lighthouse to be built to help prevent future wrecks. The Hanois (named after the reef it was built upon) was built in 1862, with engineer William Douglass overseeing the construction and it cost just over £25,000. The word Hanois means 'wraith', a type of willowy spectre in Guernsey French. It stands 36 metres high (33 metres above mean high water) and was built section by section. The Cornish granite was dressed at Castle Cornet then taken by boat to the Hanois reef, piece by piece, and dovetailed together. The lighthouse

Hanois lighthouse. (Soo Wellfair)

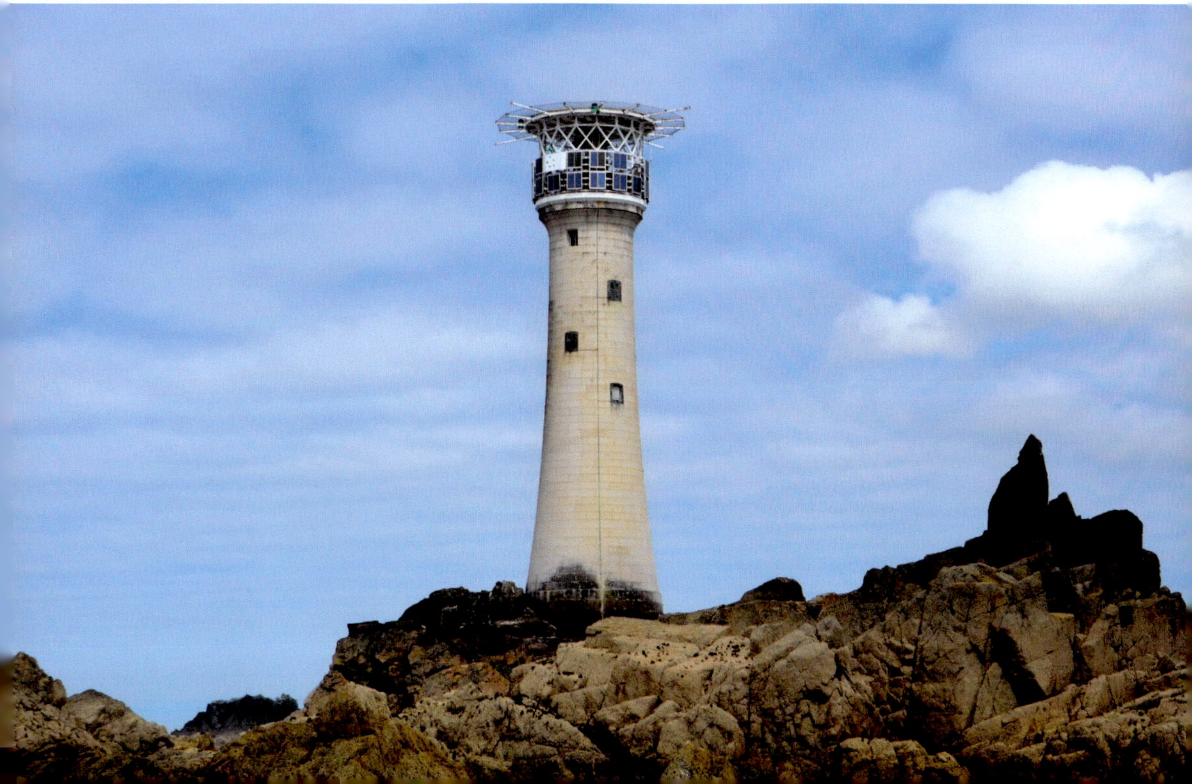

was built with seven rooms. The main rooms were 13 feet in diameter and 9 feet high. The lighthouse was manned by two crews, with three men on each crew, working a four-week tour of duty. The lighthouse keepers and their families lived in the Trinity Cottages near Portelet, and the only means of communication was by semaphore. The lighthouse has had a few modifications over the years, including the installation of a helipad above the lantern in 1979 and solar panels in the late 1990s, when the lighthouse also became fully automated. It is now monitored and controlled by Trinity House in Essex. It was the last Trinity House rock tower to be manned and is also the most southerly of all lighthouses administered by them. There is a 1-metre-tall model of the lighthouse in the Fort Grey Shipwreck Museum. The lantern of the model flashes perfectly in sync with the real lighthouse.

The only real change of use for the lighthouse came during the occupation, when the remote site was used for solitary confinement.

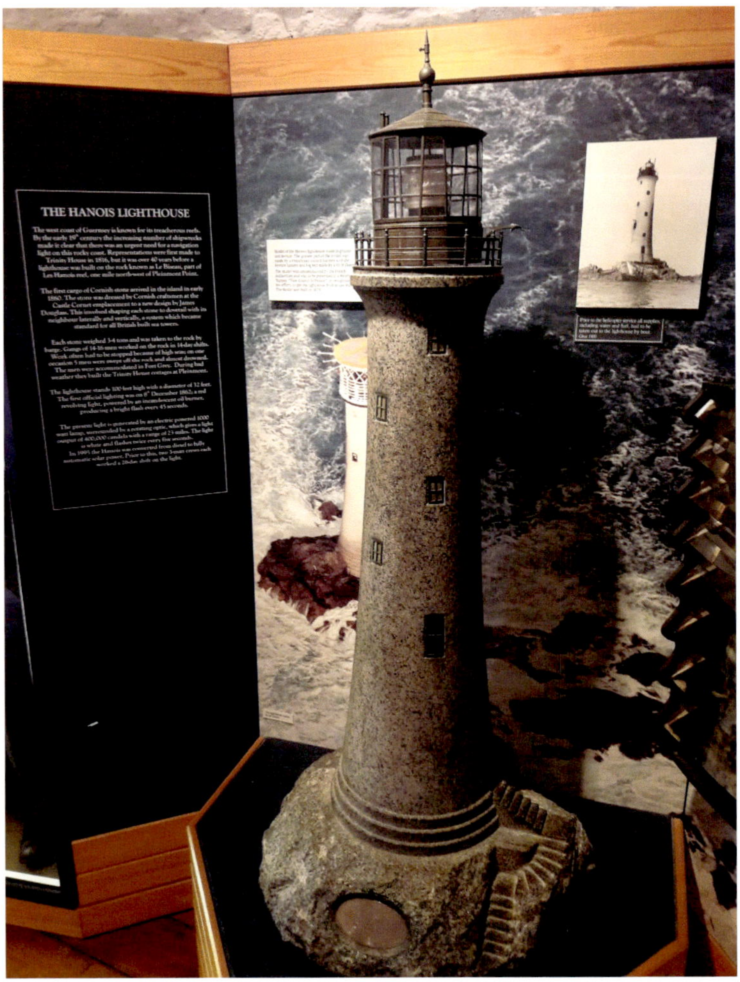

Hanois model at Fort Grey. (Soo Wellfair)

37. St Saviour's Church

The oldest part of St Saviour's dates back to the fourteenth century, although it was extensively rebuilt in the seventeenth century after being struck by lightning and badly damaged. It is believed that some parts of the church may have been reclaimed from an old French church that had burned down. It is an interesting structure with a battlemented square tower, sitting beneath an octagonal spire with an impressive 7-foot weathervane. The church has three bells, which were recast in 1634.

Like many local churches, St Saviour's is believed to have been built on the site of a much older place of worship, with several examples of Christianised menhirs (standing stones) within the grounds.

The graveyard has some rather interesting features, including an obelisk that serves as a memorial for the thirty soldiers from the parish who lost their lives during both world wars. The oldest grave in the churchyard dates back to 1602 and bears the name Nicholas Torode. Oddly, Mr Torode's headstone is presented both upside down and back to front. Another interesting burial plot is the grave of eleven Irish women lost in a cutter ship named *Pitt*, which was wrecked off Guernsey's west coast in 1819.

During the occupation St Saviour's was utilised by the occupying forces as an observation post. During this time, a vast network of tunnels was dug out beneath the churchyard, stretching as far as 700 metres. It is thought that these tunnels were originally built as ration stores and then later used to store ammunition and

St Saviour's Church. (Soo Wellfair)

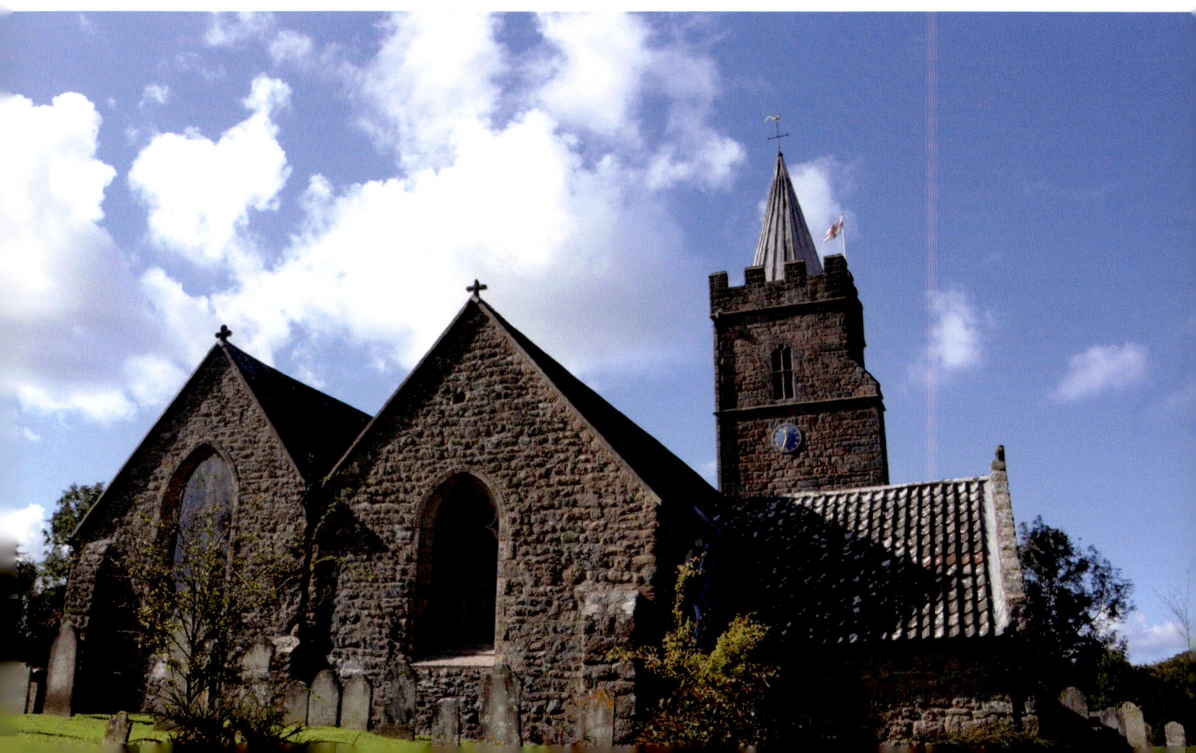

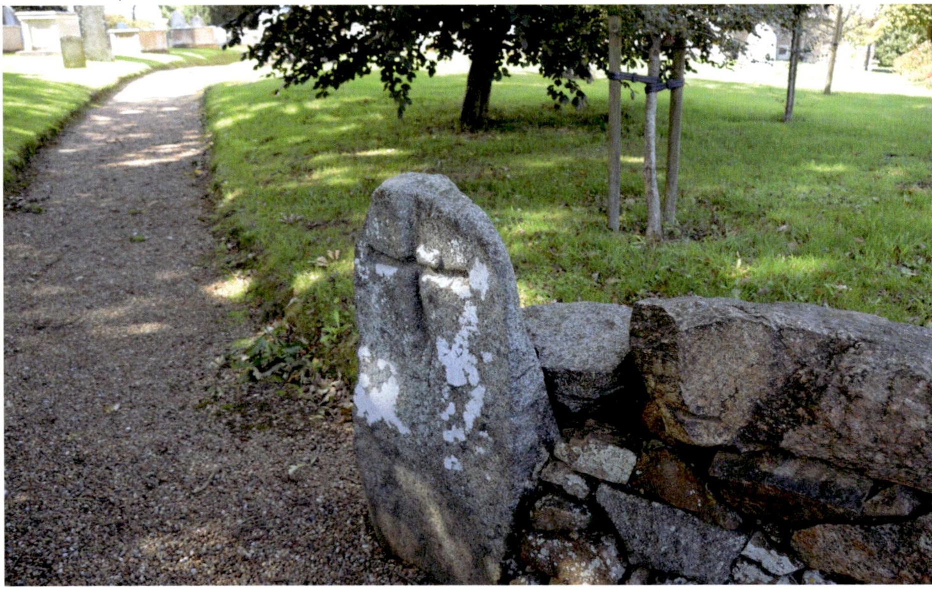

Christianised menhir. (Soo Wellfair)

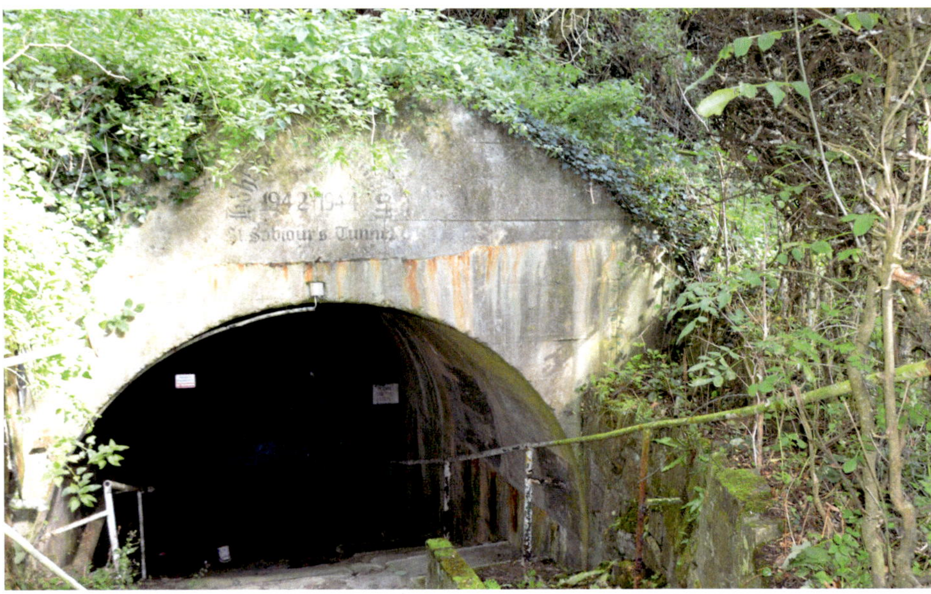

Entrance to former tunnel constructed during the occupation. (Soo Wellfair)

vehicles. Much of what was left was scrapped in the 1950s but some items were later salvaged and are on display in the German Occupation Museum and it is believed that some still remain. Much of the tunnel complex and the access points are on private land now and are inaccessible, apart from a yearly inspection from the local Douzaine (parish council).

38. St Saviour's Reservoir

The reservoir in the parish of St Saviour is probably one of the most impressive structures in Guernsey, in terms of sheer size and the level of engineering involved in designing it. Back in 1936 Guernsey Water recommended the building of a dam to help cope with an ever-growing population and need of a reliable water supply. A sum of £200,000 was allocated to the project to impound the land. The flooding of this small valley saw the loss of around six dwellings. At times when water levels in the reservoir are extremely low, the remains of the buildings in the bottom of the valley can be seen. There are also a number of ruins scattered around the edges of the reservoir, largely taken back by nature yet still a reminder of the reservoir's past.

Construction of the dam started in 1938 and it was quite a complicated project and not without its challenges. The wall was then built on the rock and concrete was pumped into it to seal the fissures. It is a gravity dam, meaning it has been designed to hold back water using the weight of the structure to resist the pressure of water pushing against it. There is also a system of drains underneath to help disperse percolating water. As concrete expands and contracts depending on the temperature and can subsequently crack, this reservoir was constructed in blocks joined by vertical copper strips, allowing flexibility. The initial design included a cladding of pink Cobo granite on the visible side of the dam, but this never went ahead as there

Reservoir dam building. (Soo Wellfair)

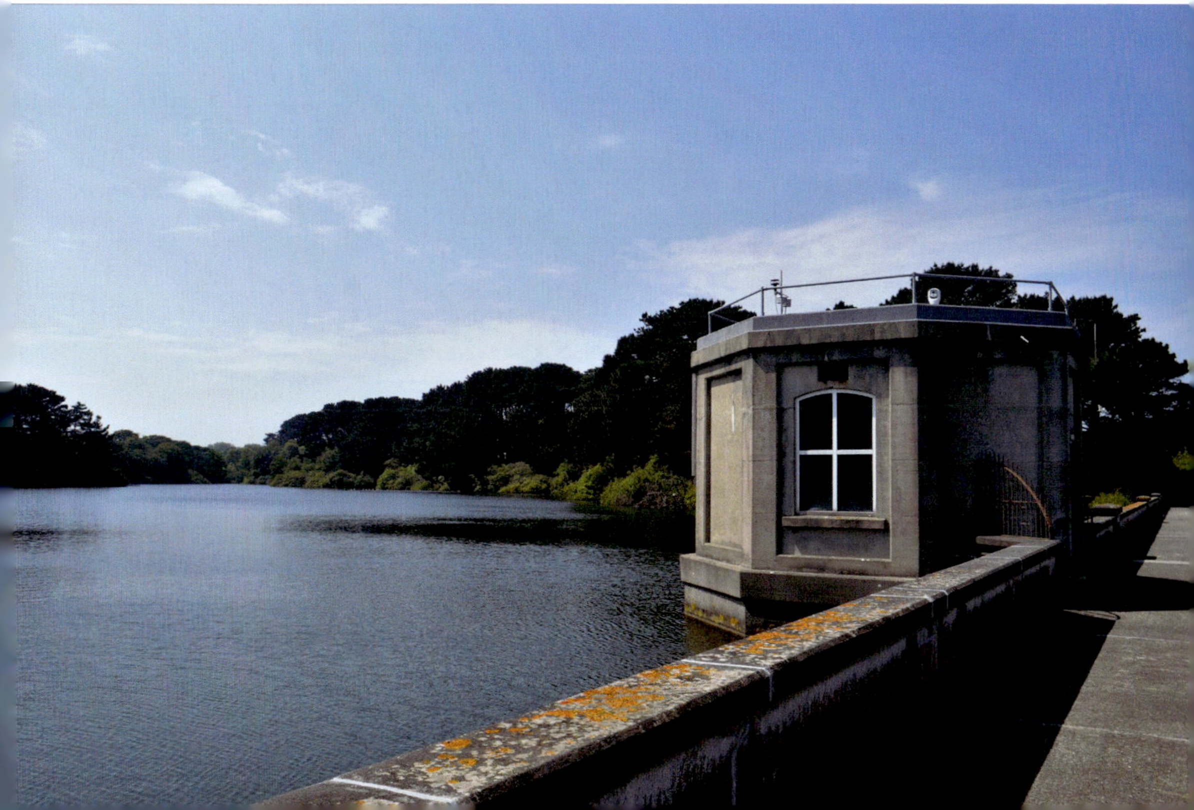

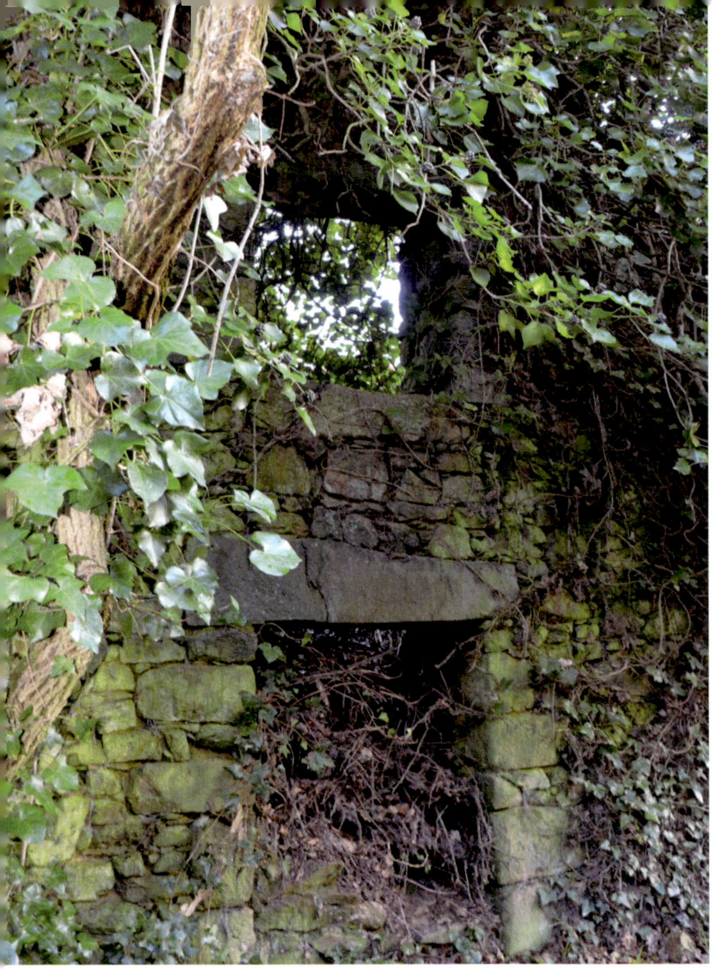

Remains of farm buildings from flooded village. (Soo Wellfair)

were not enough skilled quarrymen available at the time. Construction was held up during the Second World War but restarted afterwards and the main structure was completed in 1947. The dam was constructed using approximately 50,000 cubic metres of concrete and holds around 240,000,000 gallons of water, providing 25 per cent of the island's stored water. St Saviour's Reservoir has become a popular spot for walkers and bird-spotters and a beautiful 3-kilometre woodland trail now snakes its way around the water's edge.

39. St Andrew's Church

Considered most likely to be Guernsey's smallest parish church, St Andrew's is also located in the island's only landlocked parish. Like many churches, it is likely that it has been rebuilt at least once during its history, and probably replaced a much older pagan site long before that. This idea is supported by the existence of an ancient holy well called La Fontaine de St Clair, which can be found just across the road. One of several wells in Guernsey, these were thought to be sacred places and the water which flowed from them was believed to have curative powers. Dating

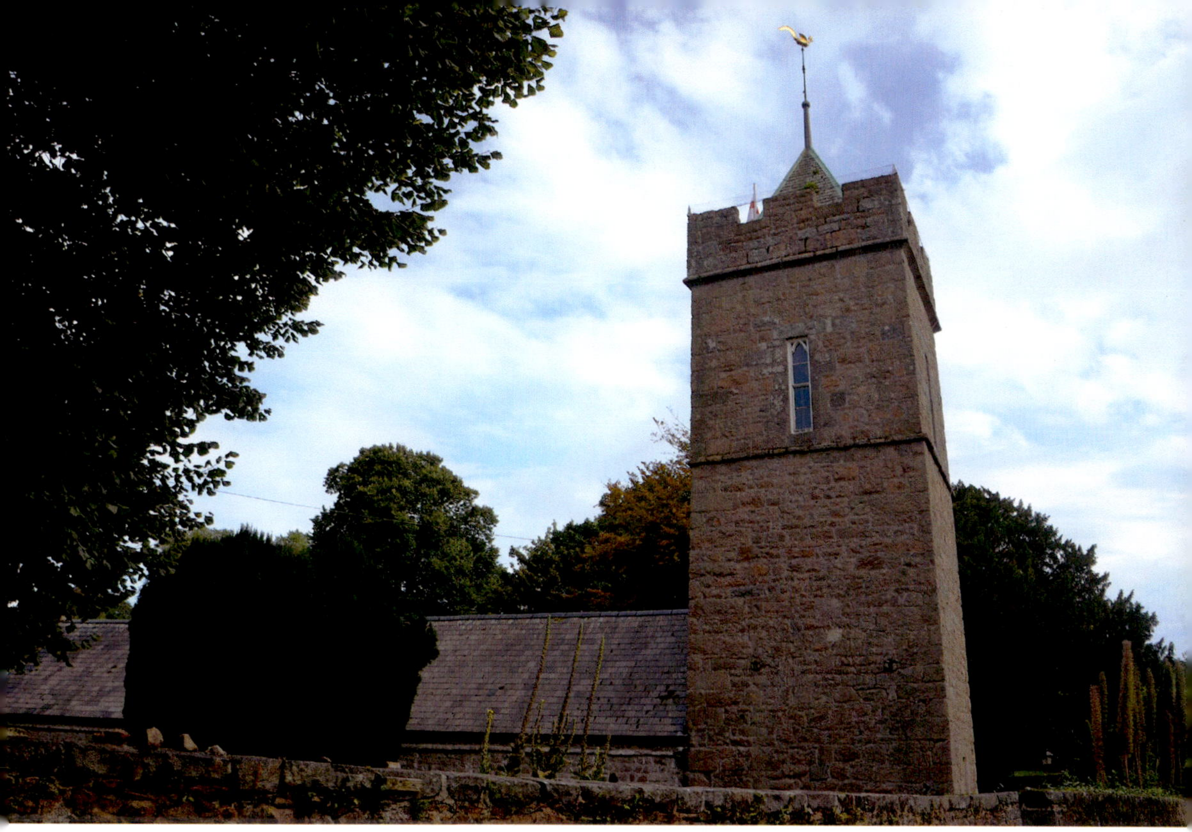

Above: St Andrew's Church. (Soo Wellfair)

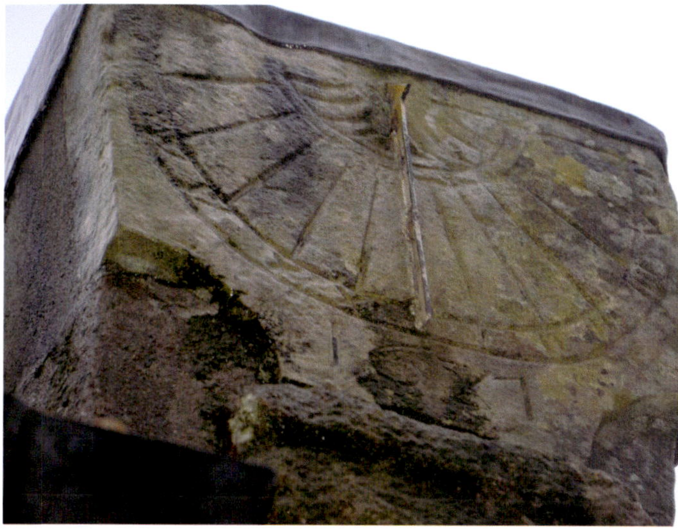

Right: Seventeenth-century sundial. (Soo Wellfair)

Guernsey's churches is always quite difficult, due to the lack of reliable parish records. It's believed that the original church, built in the eleventh century, was gifted by William, Duke of Normandy, to the Abbey of St Martin de Marmoutier and remained under French ownership until the Middle Ages. The church is also known as 'St André de la Pommeraye', which means 'St Andrew of the Apple Orchard'.

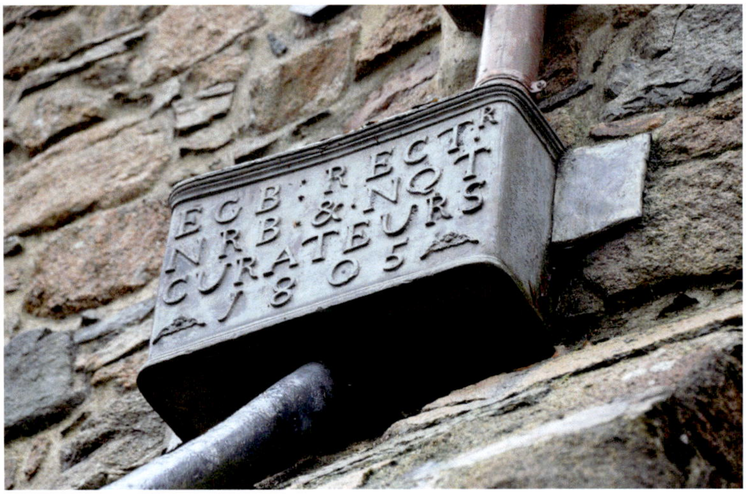

Engraved rainwater head. (Soo Wellfair)

The oldest parts of the existing church date back to the twelfth century. There is evidence to suggest that that church was almost doubled in size in the fifteenth century and greatly restored and expanded in the eighteenth century.

The church has three bells, which were cast in 1778. These bells once hung for ringing, but this is no longer the case. The bells are now rung using an Ellacombe apparatus, which uses a series of hammers to strike the stationary bells.

The present organ was installed by Norman and Beard of Norwich and London in 1902, in memory of the late Queen Victoria.

The road running alongside the church often draws the attention of passers-by, as it is named Rue des Morts. This 'Road of the Dead' goes back to days when funeral processions would have taken place.

A very old sundial, dating back to 1681, can be found on the outside of the church. It is, however, in exceptionally good condition for something that has been outside for almost 350 years and it's therefore assumed that it has been restored fairly recently.

Another quirky feature is an engraved rainwater head from 1805, which bears the names of the rector and churchwardens of the time.

40. The Little Chapel

Nestled within the beautiful valley area known as Les Vauxbelets, in the parish of St Andrew, lies the Little Chapel. Standing at just 16 × 9 feet, the Little Chapel may be small in size but it is mighty in visual impact. Based on the Rosary Basilica of Lourdes, every inch of the Little Chapel is adorned with a colourful array of broken china, seashells and pebbles, and is an absolute feast for the eyes. This form of mosaic work is known as Picassiette, which is French for 'plate stealer', and one of the most famous examples is La Maison Picassiette in Chartres, France.

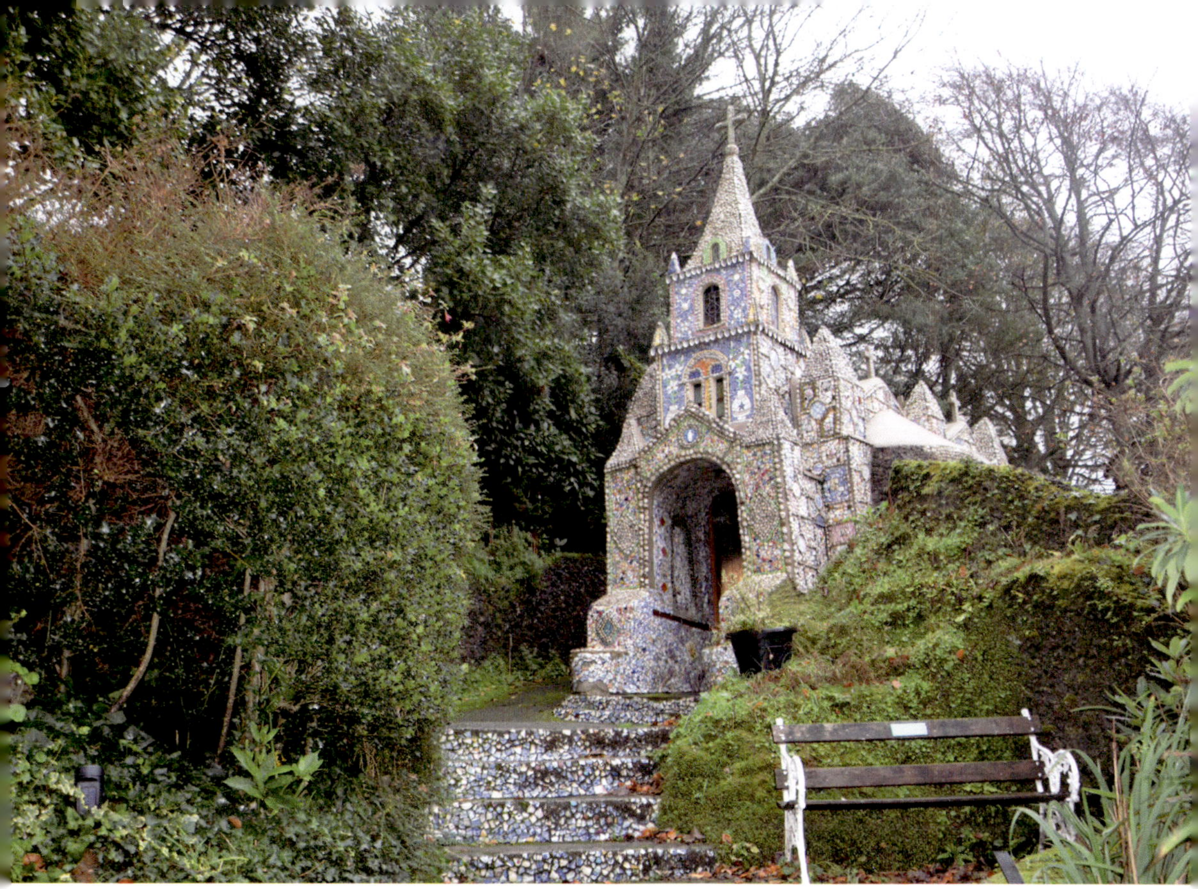

Above and below: The Little Chapel. (Soo Wellfair)

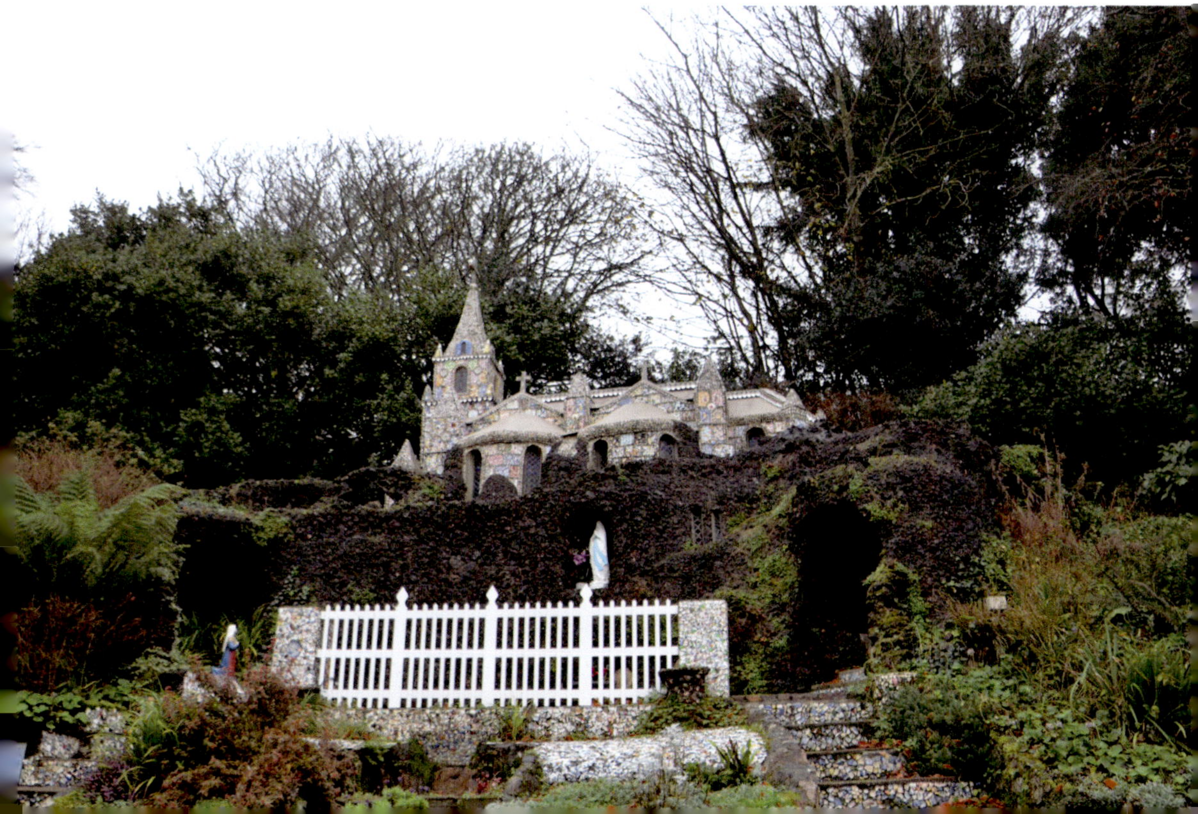

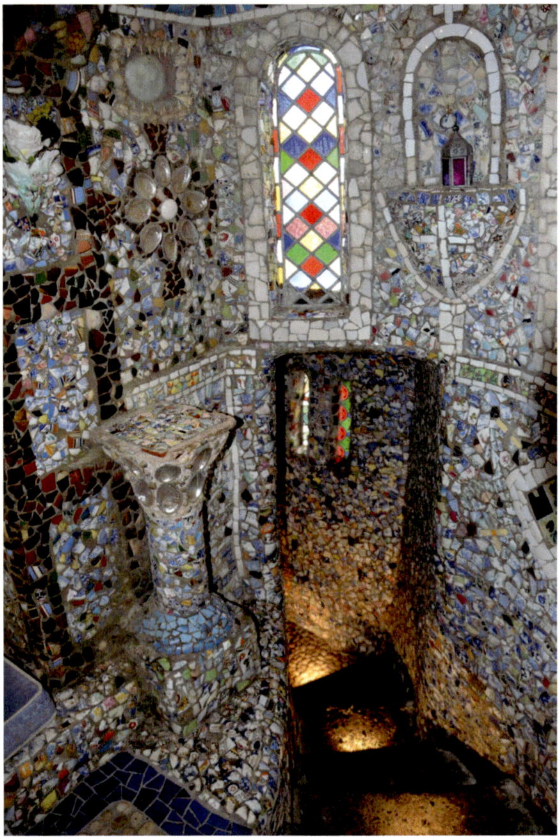

Inside the Little Chapel. (Soo Wellfair)

The version of the Little Chapel that stands today is actually the third incarnation of this stunning landmark. It was originally built in 1914 by Brother Deodat, a member of a French monastic order known as the Brothers of the Christian Schools, who had settled in Guernsey in 1904. The first version of the chapel, measuring just 9 × 4.5 feet, was pulled down within a day as Deodat has received criticism for its small size! Soon after, Deodat completed a second, larger version, but even though – at 9 × 6 feet – it was larger than its predecessor, it was destroyed in 1923 after the Bishop of Portsmouth was unable to fit through the doorway. And so, the building of the third and final version began. The main shell of the building, now measuring 16 × 9 feet, took just two years to complete. However, the decoration would continue for many years. Sadly, Brother Deodat was unable to finish his project due to ill health, and returned to France just before the Second World War. Another member of the order, Brother Cephas, took over the decoration of the Little Chapel until his retirement in 1965. The Little Chapel is a very popular attraction for both visitors and locals, and it never fails to impress. It is a beautiful part of the landscape and its form and colours can be admired from some distance. Yet it is when you get up close, that you can really appreciate the intricacy and variety of all the individual pieces that make up this unique landmark. In 2017 the chapel was gifted to a charitable trust who embarked on an extensive restoration project. The almost 100-year-old building was starting to show some structural weakness and at a cost of £500,000 was underpinned and stabilised. The recent restoration also uncovered the original clinker base to the chapel. This was a byproduct they came about by burning fossil fuels to heat greenhouses, back in Guernsey's great tomato-growing years.

42. Monnaie Chapel

The Chapel of Christ the Healer, known better locally as the Monnaie Chapel, has been the only Christian chapel dedicated to the Ministry of Healing in the Channel Islands since it was consecrated in 1957.

The chapel was the vision of the Drake family, who had sadly lost their son Robin to cancer at the young age of twenty-four. Before Robin's passing, his father, Revd Frank Drake, having spent time at a Christian healing centre in the UK, felt it was his calling to build a small chapel at home in Guernsey. It was something of a community project, and was designed, built and funded locally. It is still used for weekly services, attended by a small yet dedicated local congregation.

It is not intended as a 'tourist attraction', yet very much has an open-door policy for those who wish to quietly use the chapel for prayer and contemplation and to admire the chapel's many beautiful features.

Monnaie Chapel. (Soo Wellfair)

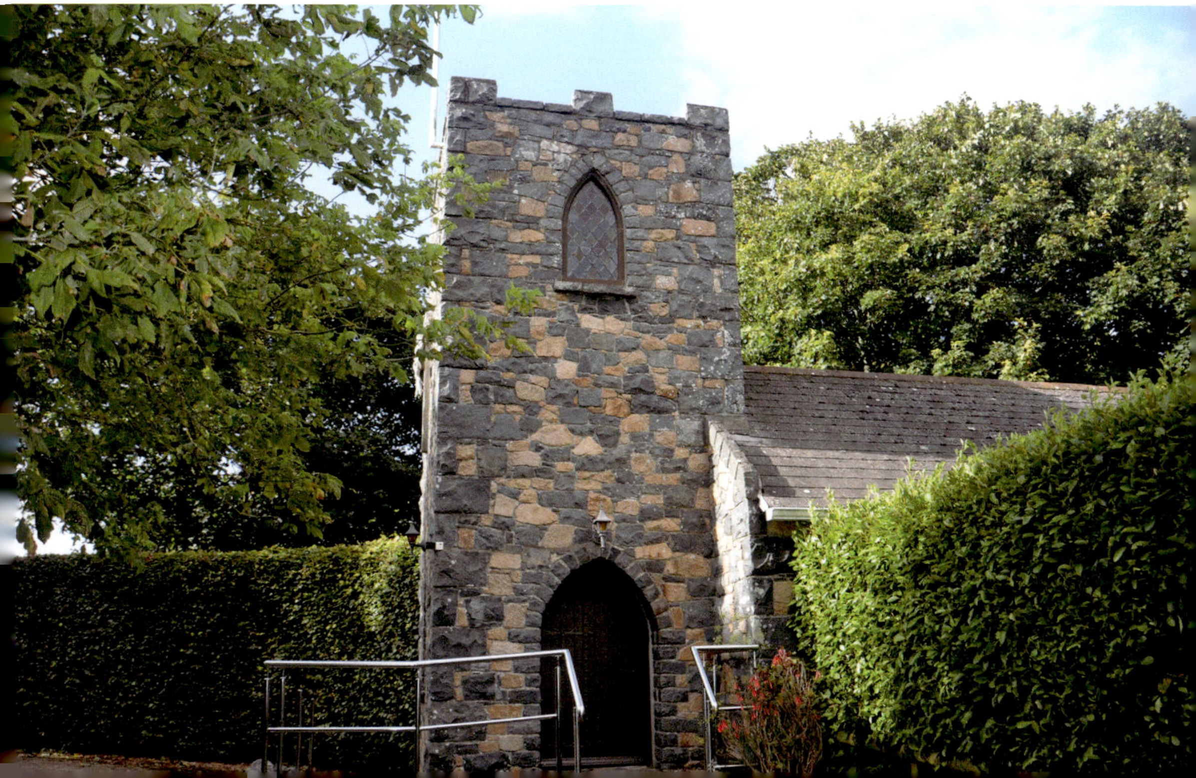

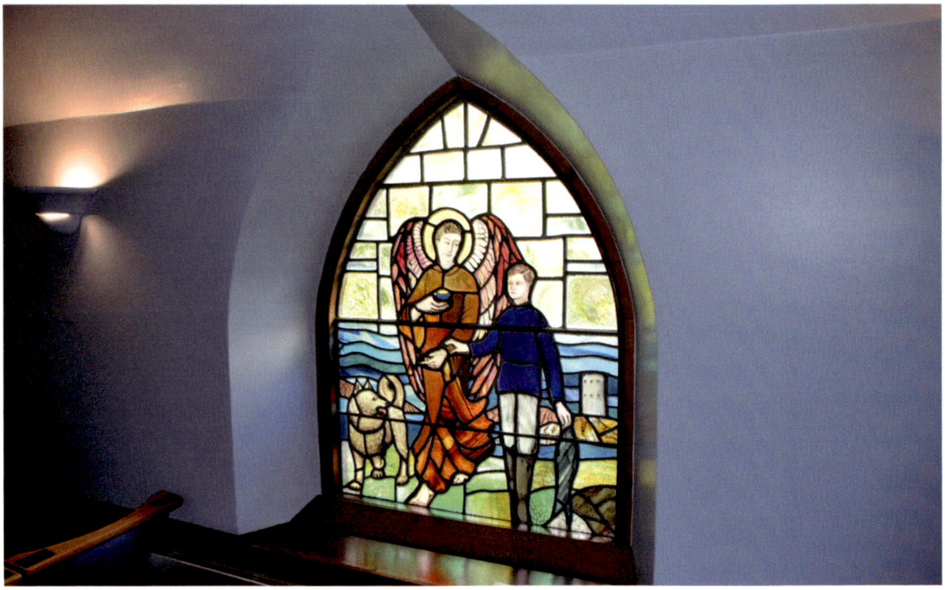

Stained-glass window depicting Tobias. (Soo Wellfair)

A local stained-glass artist, Mary Eily de Putron, designed and made the chapel's beautiful windows. One window in particular is especially eye-catching, depicting the story of Raphael, the Archangel of Healing. With him are Tobias and his dog, with the former wearing a traditional Guernsey jumper (known as a 'guernsey') and in the background you'll spot one of the island's iconic eighteenth-century loophole towers.

Outside the chapel you will find an impressive carved wooden crucifix. This was created by the well-known German sculptor Faust Lang. Lang was known for using a lot of detail in his work, giving more definition to facial features, hair, muscles, and so on to create a more lifelike effect.

43. German Underground Hospital

The German Underground Hospital is the largest tunnel complex built in Guernsey during the occupation, with around 1,000,000 cubic feet of rock removed over a time period of around three and a half years. It was largely completed using forced labour and work conditions would have been extremely taxing both physically and mentally. There are about 1.25 miles worth of tunnels and an area of around 75,000 square feet. It was built under a hill and is practically invisible other than the main access points. It was originally built as a personnel shelter but was later used as an ammunition store and hospital. These two areas are joined by interconnecting tunnels, but the ammunition store is larger than the hospital area. The hospital was ready for use by 1944, but

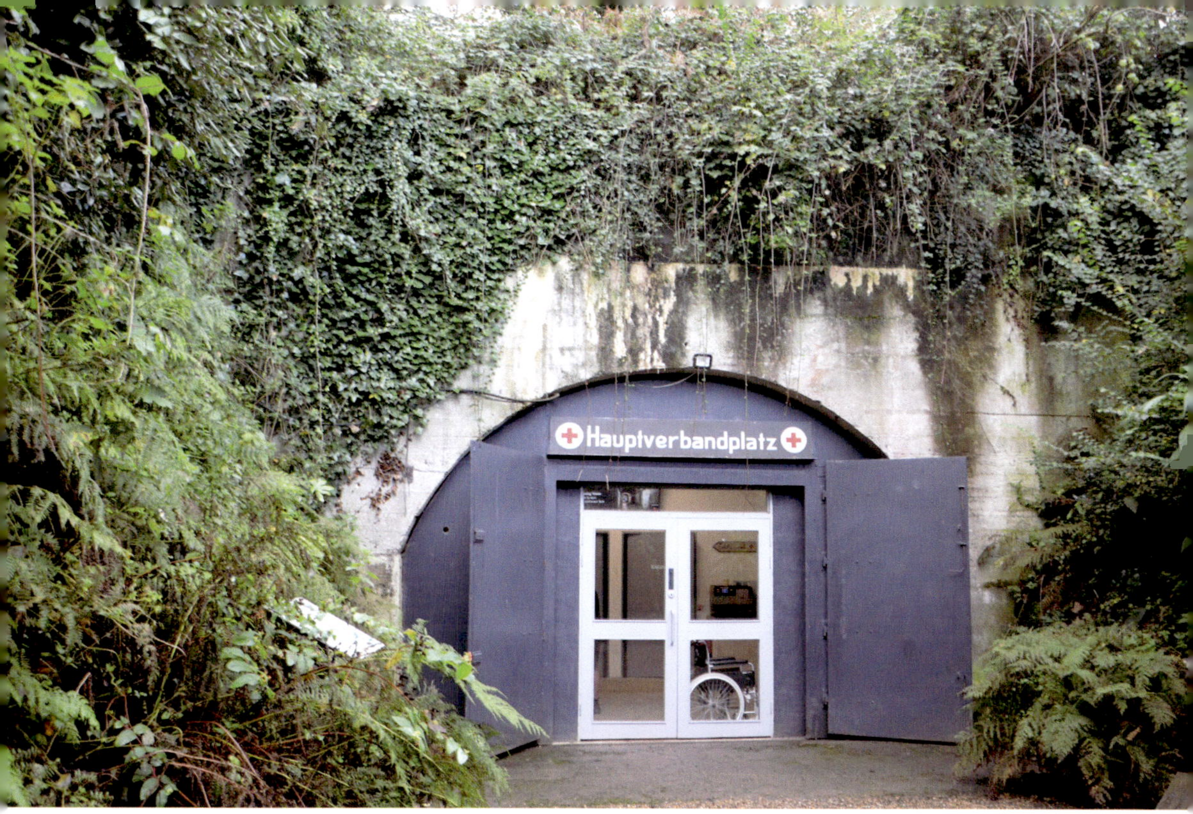

Above: German Underground Hospital. (Soo Wellfair)

Below: One of the Underground Hospital's many tunnels. (Soo Wellfair)

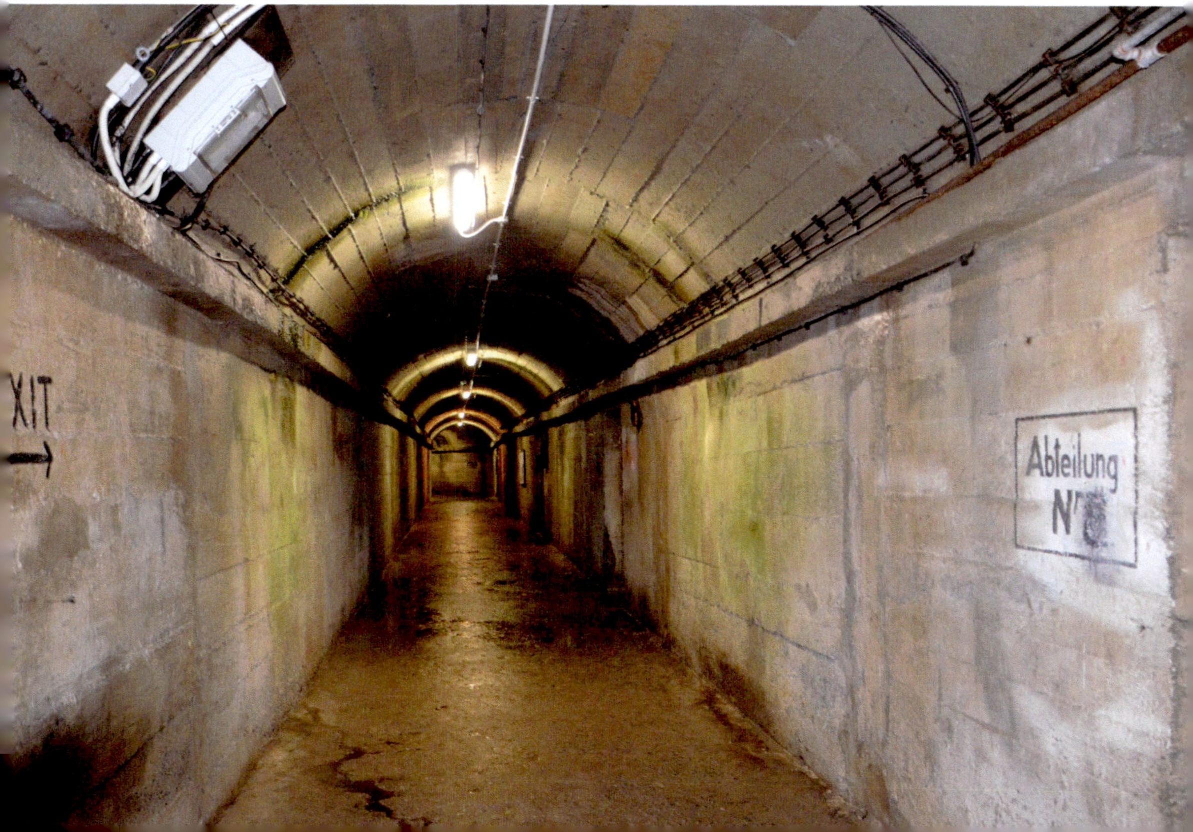

the tunnels were never fully finished, and it is possible to view these unfinished tunnels should you visit the site. The hospital never really fulfilled its intended purpose. In fact, it was used for less than three months in 1944 when troops were moved to Guernsey after being injured in an allied attack in France. The conditions were far from ideal, and these patients were moved elsewhere after around ten weeks.

The site was recently taken over in 2018 by a voluntary organisation called Festung Guernsey, who maintain and preserve the island's Second World War fortifications. They have done a lot of work to improve the visitor experience, whilst maintaining the atmosphere of a vast heritage site which has changed very little over the years. Visitors are always advised to wear something warm and waterproof as the tunnels are cold and wet, which makes a visit a truly immersive experience. As well as being open as a museum, the site is also used for various events throughout the year, including live music and theatre performances. It has also been used over the years as a film set, featuring in the 1973 war film *The Blockhouse* and more recently the 2023 found-footage film, *Underground*.

44. St Apolline's Chapel

Tucked away in the parish of St Saviour is St Apolline's Chapel, dedicated to St Apolline (also known as Apollina or Appolonia). Apolline was a Christian deaconess in the third century. Living under Roman rule in Alexandria, she was punished for providing shelter for persecuted Christians. She was beaten so badly that all of her teeth were either broken or knocked out, and when soldiers threatened to throw her onto a fire if she did not renounce her faith, she threw herself into the flames. She was made a martyr and St Apolline, patron saint of dentists. There is a window in the chapel dedicated to her that depicts her being looked over by an angel holding a tooth.

The chapel was built in the late fourteenth century as a private chapel, then fell out of use after the Reformation. It was used as a stable until it was purchased in the late nineteenth century by the States for £120 and has now been a protected building since 1938. It was the first building in Guernsey to be purchased by the States in order to preserve it. The chapel is built largely from local Guernsey granite, although there are also examples of Chausey and Caen stone being used – both from Normandy.

It is an attractive building, which can accommodate around sixteen worshippers at one time. One of the most unique features within the chapel are the medieval frescoes depicting the Last Supper and Jesus washing the feet of the Apostles. These historical works of art are extremely rare and part of what makes this little chapel a very special place to visit.

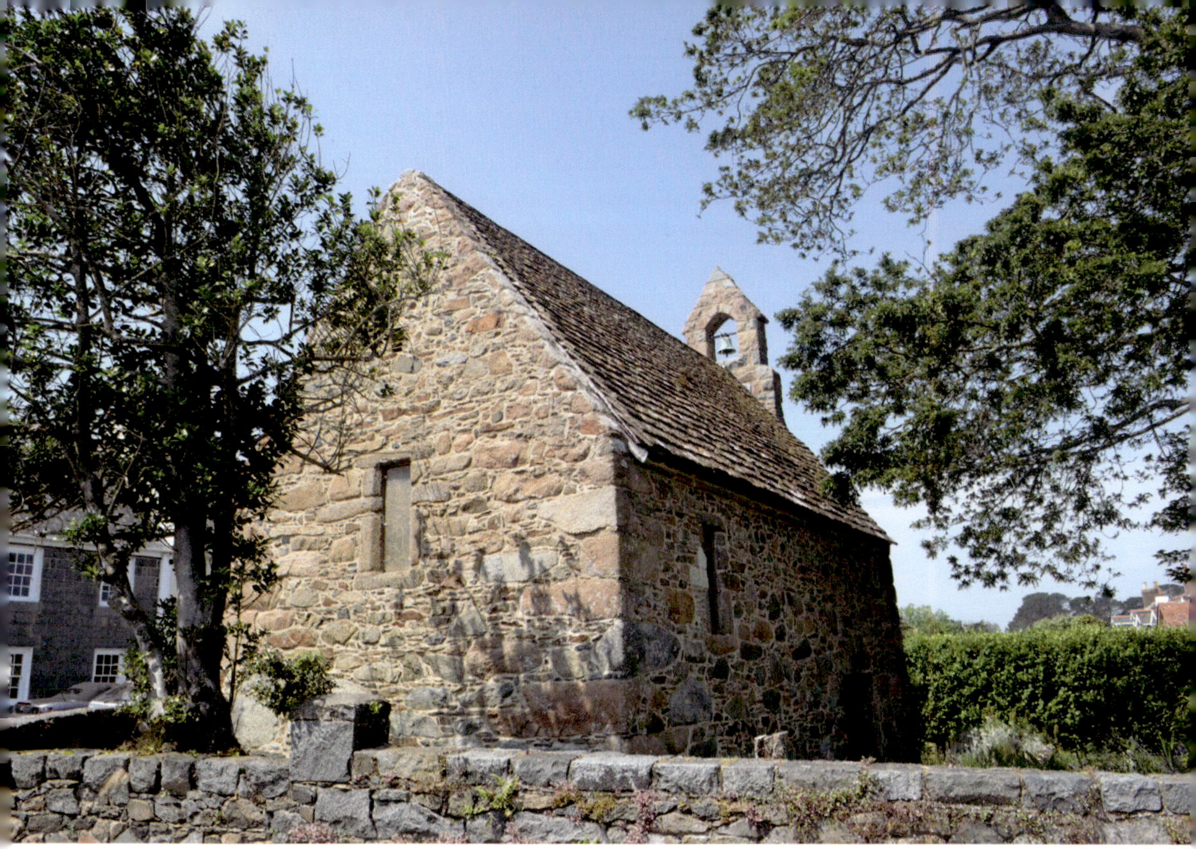

Above: St Apolline's Chapel. (Soo Wellfair)

Below: Medieval fresco. (Soo Wellfair)

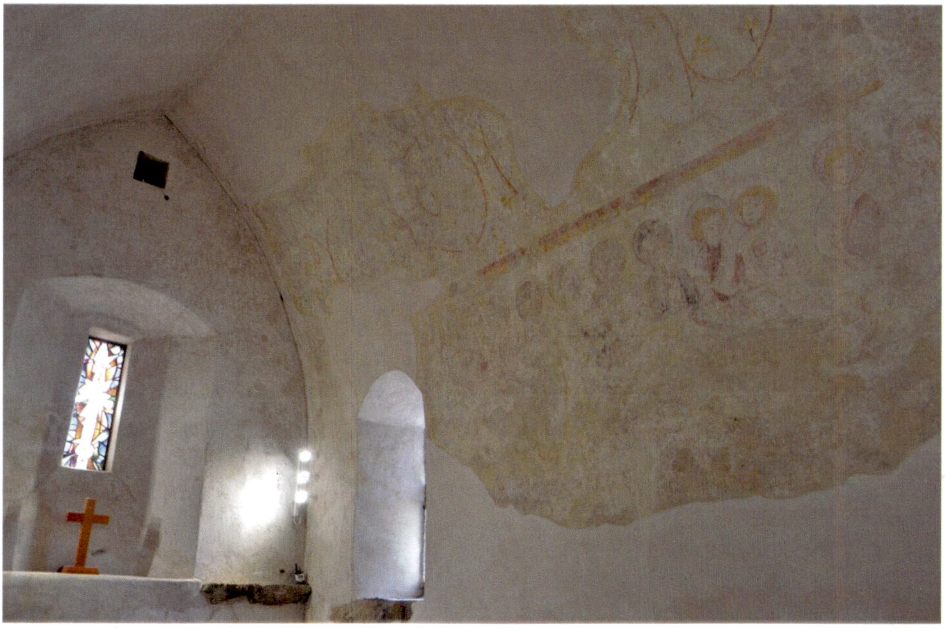

45. Castel Church

The parish church of Castel, or the church of St Marie du Castel, was built in the twelfth century under the patronage of the Abbey of Mont St Michel but has been extended and altered throughout the centuries. It is believed that the church stands on the site of a former castle or fort, constructed in the eleventh century by a piratical invader known as the Grand Geffroy or Le Grand Sarazin. The name 'Castel' may be a reference to this, and the hilltop location would certainly have provided a sound location for any defensive fortification. It is also worth noting that an older name for the church was thought to be Our Lady of Deliverance of the Castle, which may have also been the full name of the parish before being shortened, eventually becoming Castel.

An interesting feature inside the church are three medieval frescoes depicting the Last Supper, the legend of Des Trois Morts et Des Trois Vifs (The Three Dead and Three Alive) and a cloaked figure thought to be either Mary Magdalene or St Thomas Becket.

The church's organ was built in 1903 and rebuilt in 1952. The church's trio of bells was recast in 1811.

In 1999 when some work was being carried out on the church, what is now believed to have once been a seventeenth-century bell-casting pit was uncovered and is now viable to visitors through a glass window in the church floor.

Castel Church. (Soo Wellfair)

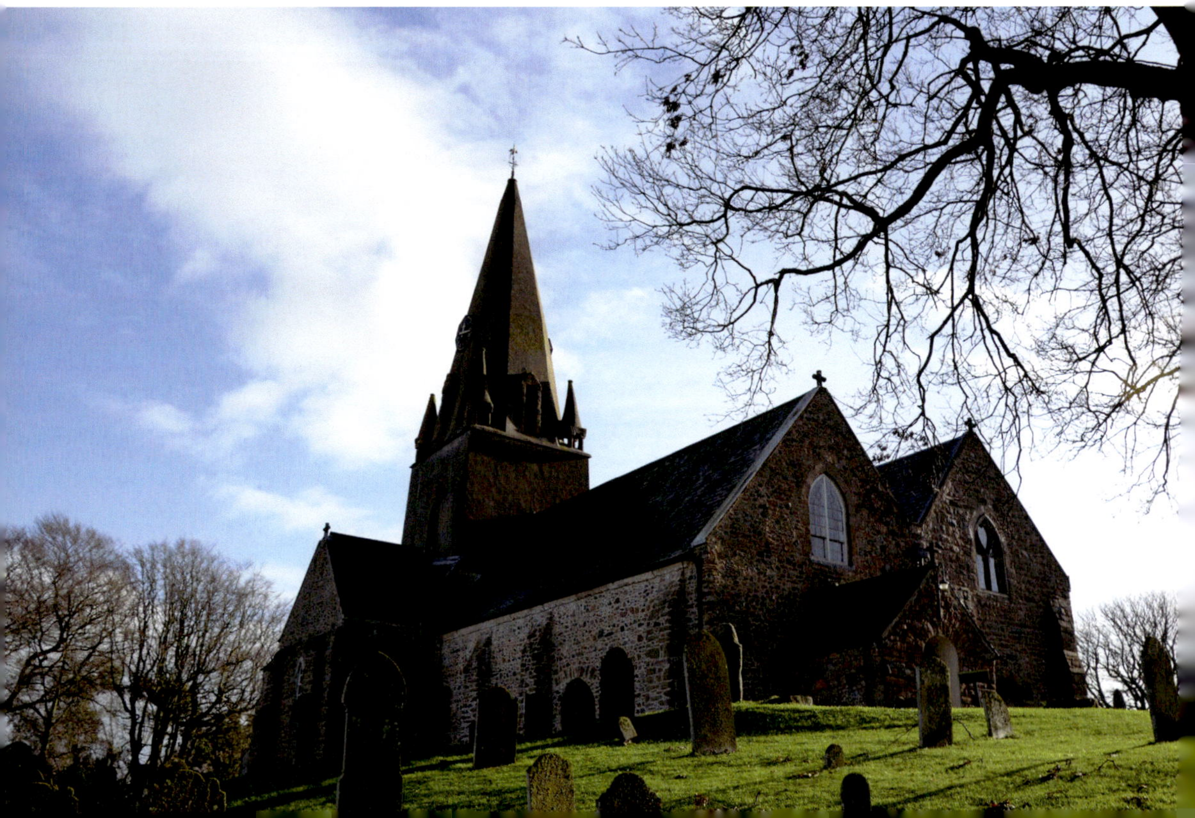

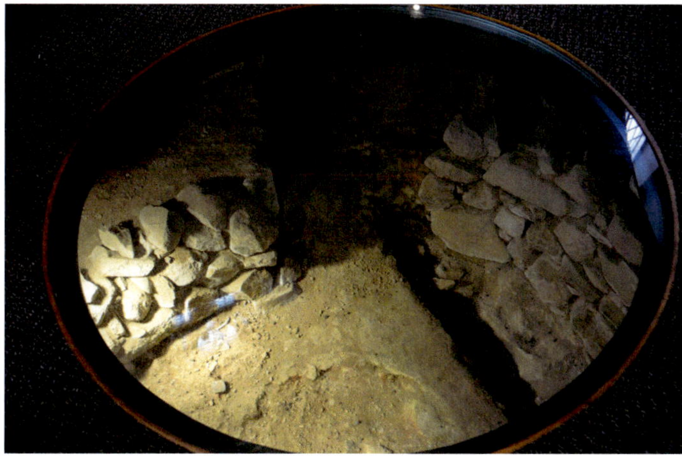

Bell-casting pit. (Soo Wellfair)

Outside, you will find a Neolithic menhir nestled among the gravestones of the cemetery. Much like its counterpart at St Martin's Church (although older by 300–400 years), the menhir has been carved to resemble the figure of a Mother Goddess. Standing at around 6 feet and 6 inches tall and over 2 feet wide, she is a striking feature of the church's grounds, but she was not always in her current position. She was found buried beneath the chancel in 1878 and thought to have been there since as early as the sixth century.

Another notable feature outside the church is a stone water trough, carved with two faces representing the sun and the moon, which dates back to the late sixteenth or early seventeenth century.

46. Repurposed Second World War Bunkers

During the occupation, hundreds of bunkers with various uses were built around Guernsey. Many of these are still very visible today, others have been concealed over the years and a small number have been either restored or repurposed.

In St Peter Port you will find the German Naval Signals Headquarters. The headquarters were used as a command centre of the German Naval Commander of the Channel Islands during the occupation. They were initially based in the hotel next door, but eventually a permanent bunker was specially built within the hotel grounds. All important radio signals being transmitted to and from Guernsey were handled here. They were even using Enigma coding machines, which were famously decoded by the staff at Bletchley Park in the UK. The bunker has been restored faithfully, with many of the original fittings still in place and is open to the public. The exhibits and rooms have been recreated with first hand advice from former German personnel, including the Naval Signals Officer.

A former searchlight bunker located on the Fort Hommet headland on the west coast, is now better known as the Shrine of the Sacred Heart. Back in the 1960s a local man named Hubert Le Galloudec asked for permission to take on the old,

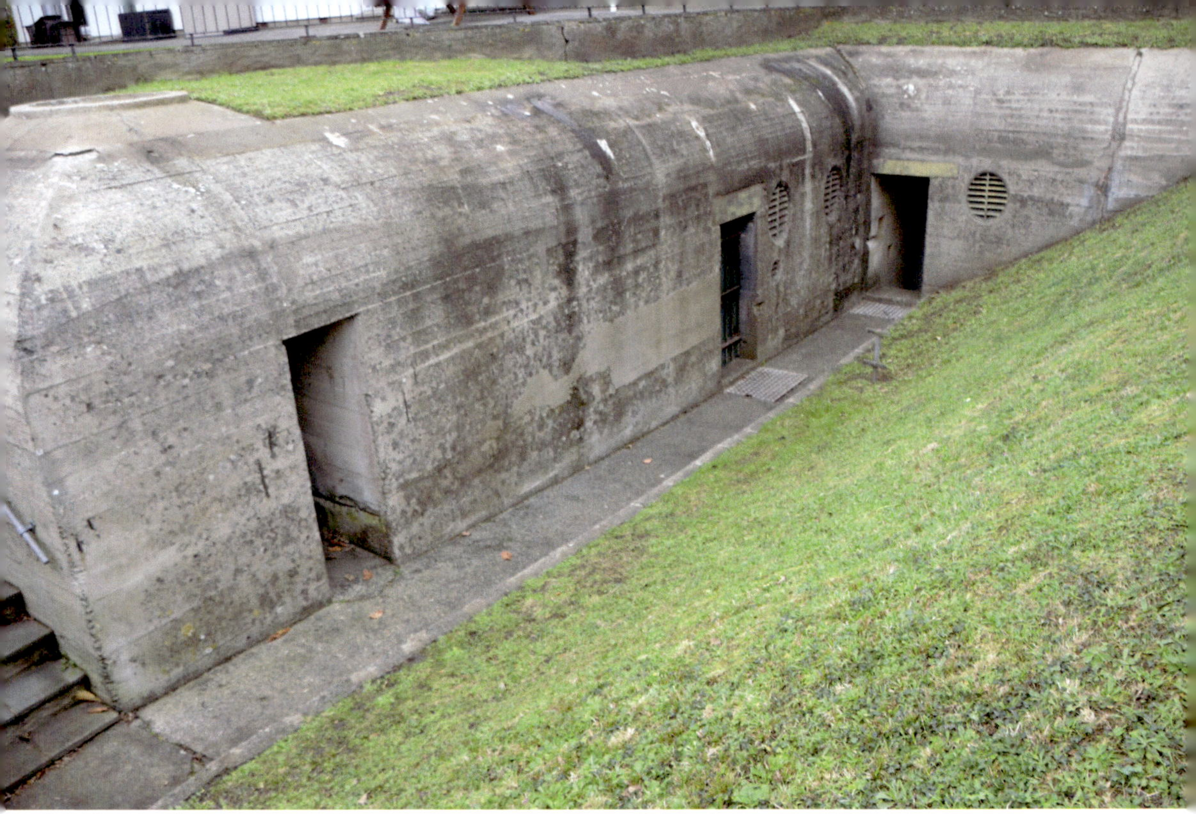

Above: Naval Signals Headquarters. (Soo Wellfair)

Below: The Shrine of the Sacred Heart. (Soo Wellfair)

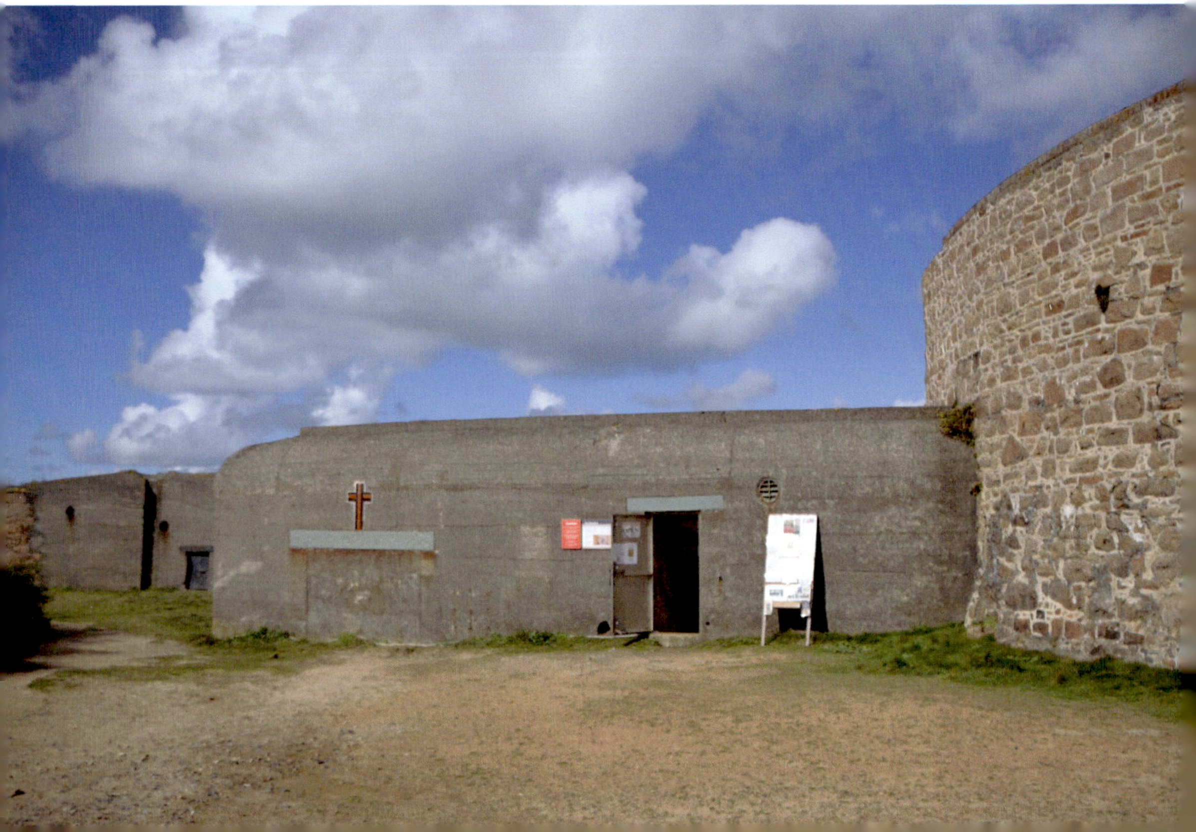

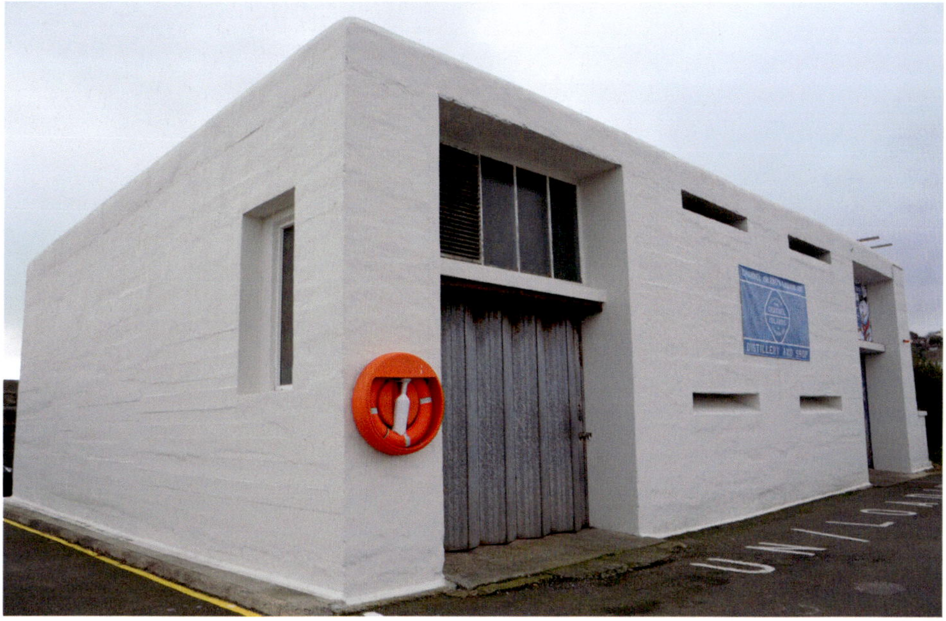

The Vivier bunker. (Soo Wellfair)

abandoned bunker and create a place of peace from a place of war in the form of a beautiful shell shrine. With the help of his wife, Maisie, Bert created over thirty murals depicting scenes from the Holy Bible, all created using shells from the local beaches. It was an arduous task taking many years and sadly was never finished as the shrine was closed down in the 1970s after becoming a target for vandals and the bunker was left abandoned for decades. In 2005 an extensive restoration of the site began, and the Shrine of the Sacred Heart was reopened in 2008.

Not far from St Peter Port's Castle Cornet you will find the Vivier bunker. This is quite an unusually spacious and tall bunker as it was originally built during the Second World War to store a large power generator and fuel. Years later it became known as the Vivier bunker, when it was used by local fishermen to store their daily catch. A vivier is a system used to keep fish and shellfish alive outside of their natural environment. The Vivier bunker now has an entirely new purpose. In 2024 it became the home of the Channel Islands Liquor Company and the rather impressive-looking copper distillery, where the famous Wheadon's Gin is made.

47. Loophole Towers

Built between 1778 and 1779, fifteen loophole towers were constructed to the same specifications. Each was 30 feet high and 20 feet wide with three floors. Loopholes were cut into the two upper floors which were designed to be used for musket fire, then a hatch led up to the roof of the tower where a small 12-pound carronade was fixed.

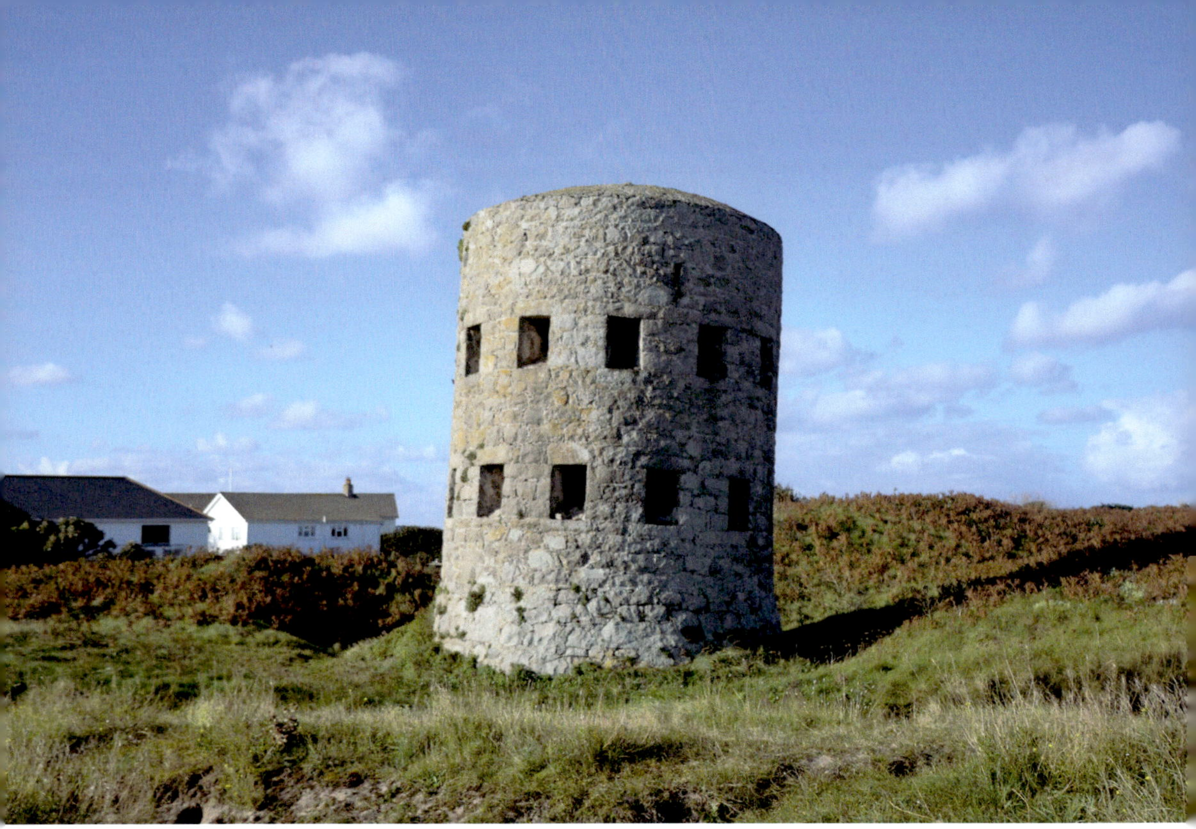

Above: The 'wonky' loophole Tower 9. (Soo Wellfair)

Below: Rousse Tower. (Soo Wellfair)

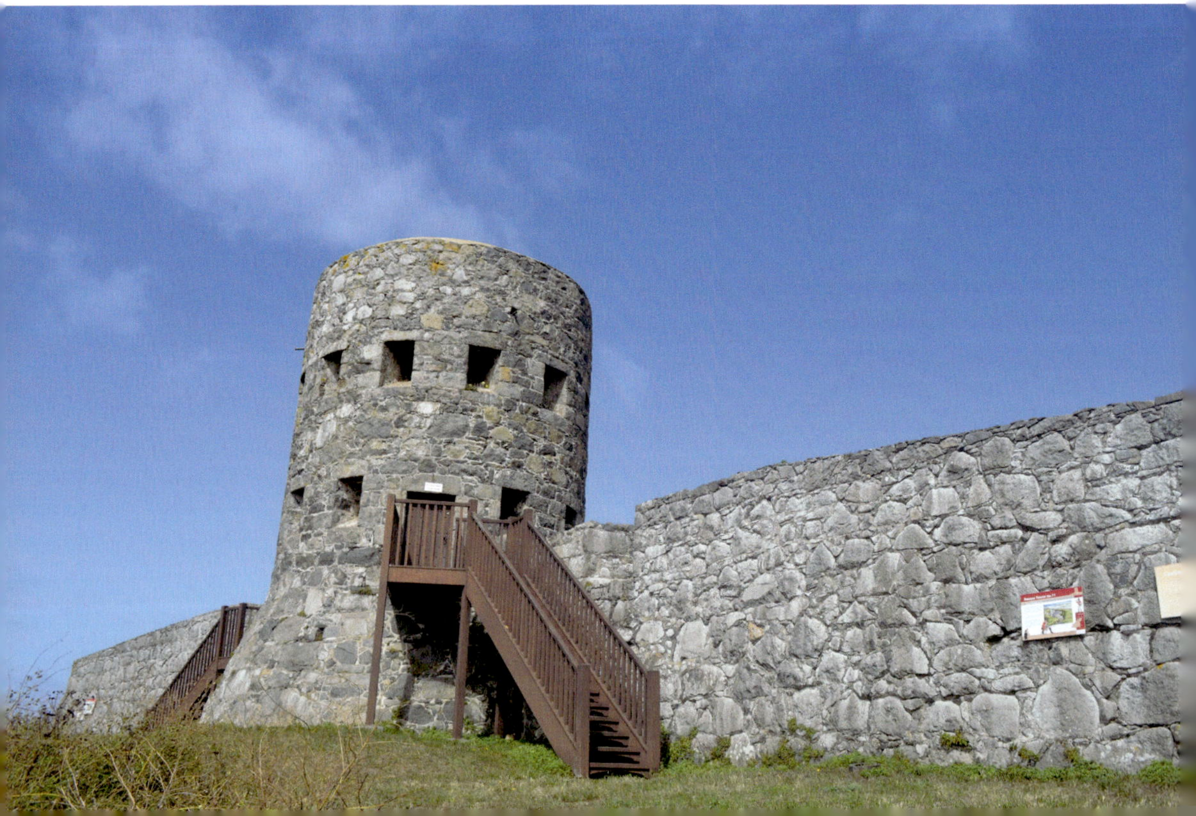

The loophole towers were manned by the Royal Guernsey Militia, which was made up of local Guernseymen. Service was compulsory, unpaid and usually undertaken on top of a full-time job.

Of the fifteen towers built, twelve still remain. Tower 1 was destroyed in 1905 to make way for tram sheds, Tower 2 was knocked down in the 1950s to make way for housing and Tower 8, on L'Ancresse Common, was destroyed during the occupation as it blocked the path of a strategic gun placement.

Although the towers were built to a certain design, they were not all identical. The granite used was sourced nearby so the stone could vary slightly, depending on the location of the tower. Tower 11, better known as Rousse Tower, was the only loophole tower built with a full-sized gun battery as part of the main tower design, instead of having a separate gun battery nearby. Tower 9 also looks a little different; it doesn't stand as straight as the others and has developed a noticeable lean. There is an urban myth that, due to its design flaw, this particular tower was never paid for.

Many of the towers are empty and no longer used. However, the towers at Rousse, Saint's Bay and Petit Port have all been restored and have at different times been open to the public. The tower at Fermain is owned by the National Trust of Guernsey and is operated as self-catering accommodation.

48. Guernsey's Three Martello Towers

On the west coast of Guernsey you will find three towers that once would have looked very similar, but now look very different indeed. Fort Grey, Fort Saumarez and Fort Hommet were all built in 1804 to help improve the island's coastal defences after the onset of the Napoleonic Wars. The name 'Martello' is believed to derive from an area of Corsica called Mortella Point, which had a defensive tower, the design of which greatly impressed the British army. The design was recreated in England and then the Channel Islands, albeit with slightly different specifications. Fort Grey is the largest, standing at 26 feet, with Fort Saumarez and Fort Hommet both about a foot shorter. They are all made from a combination of brick and local granite and cost at least half the price of their English counterparts, which raised many questions about the quality of build and suitability. However, all three have stood the test of time. The most striking thing about them now is just how different the three towers look in the twenty-first century. Fort Grey has become one of Guernsey's most recognisable landmarks, known colloquially as 'the Cup and Saucer'. The Martello tower is painted bright white and is the home to the popular Shipwreck Museum. Fort Saumarez was modified by the occupying forces during the Second World War. During this period a four-storey observation tower was built on top of the Martello tower which is now barely visible. This tower is now on private land but still very much visible on the western coastline. Fort Hommet was also dramatically altered during the occupation.

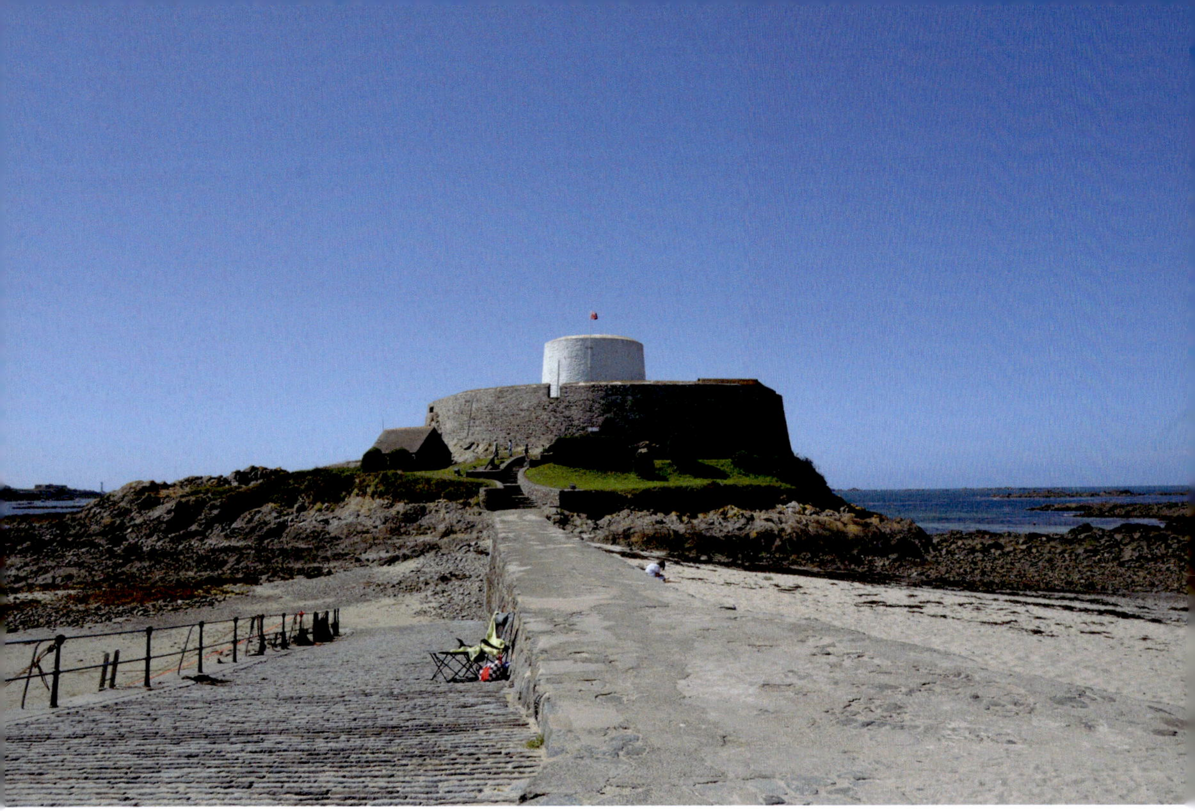

Above: Fort Grey. (Soo Wellfair)

Below: Fort Saumarez. (Soo Wellfair)

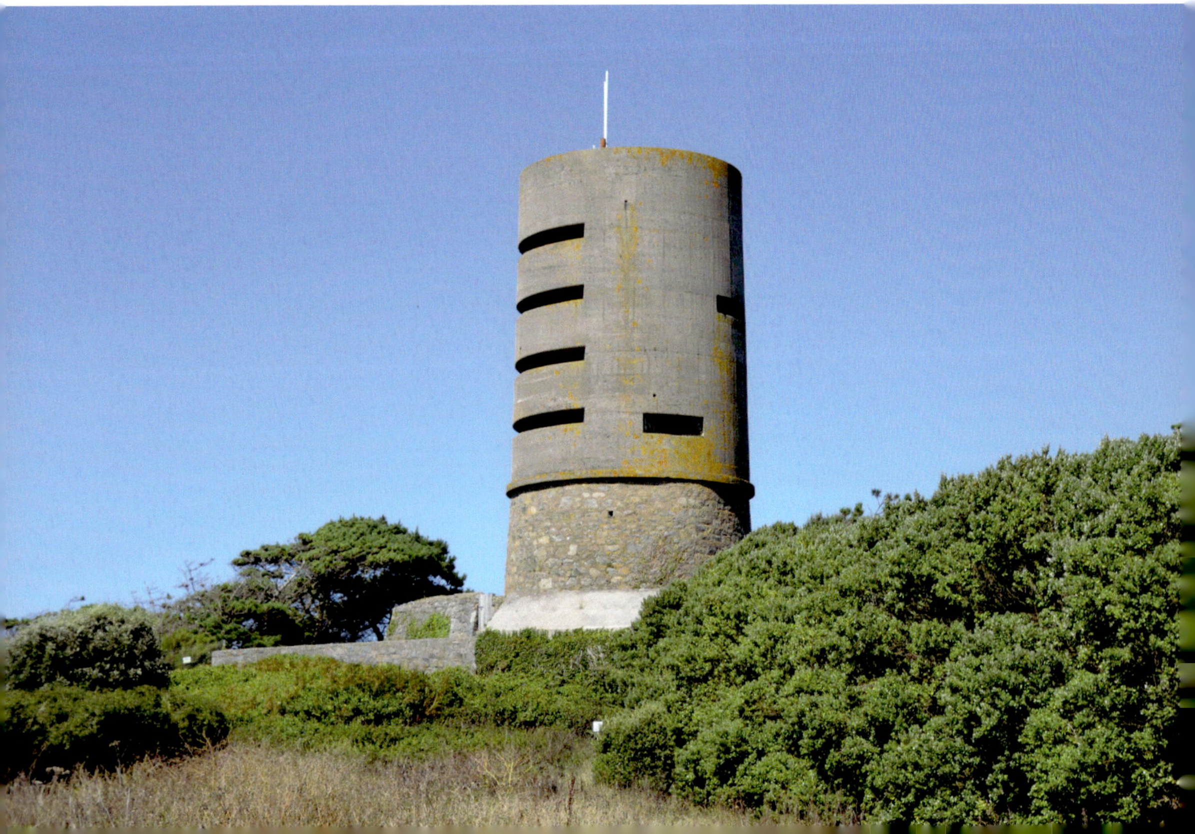

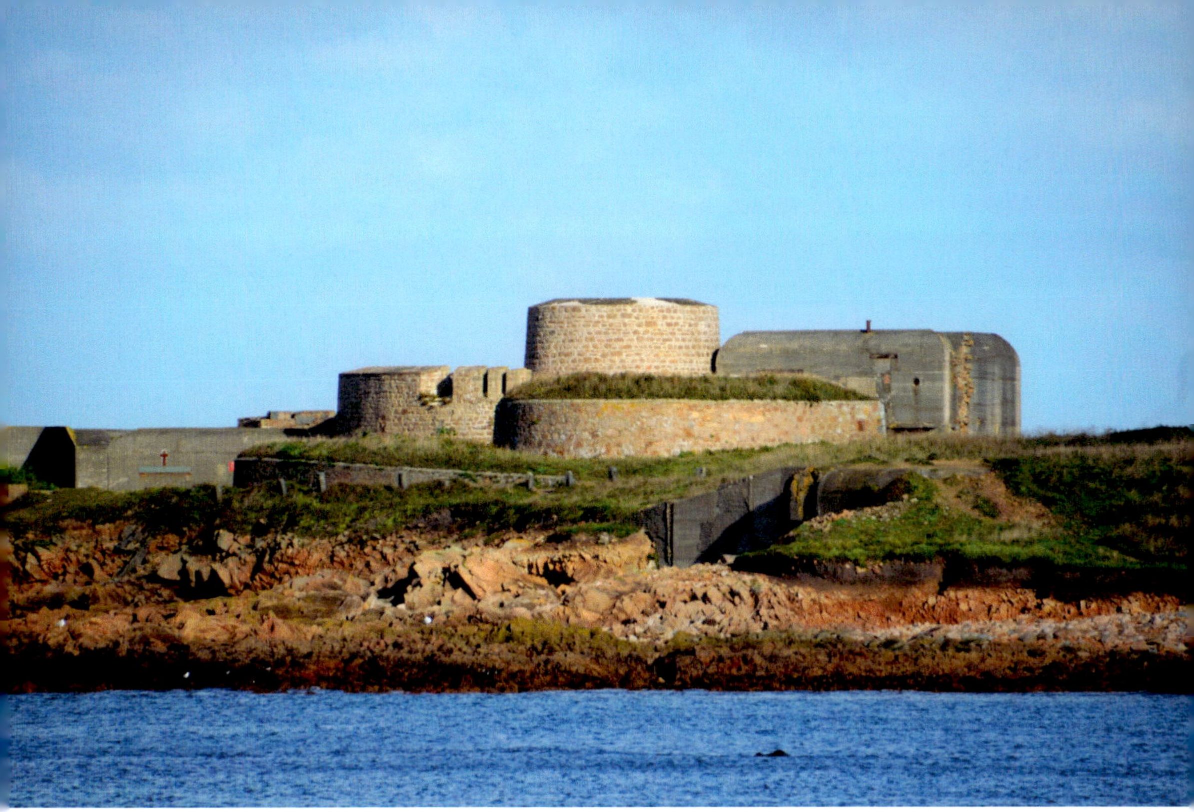

Fort Hommet. (Soo Wellfair)

49. Guernsey Glasshouses

It was once said that if you were to have flown over Guernsey in an aeroplane during the mid-twentieth century, it may have looked like a sheet of ice or, indeed, glass. This would have been due to the sheer volume of greenhouses, known better locally as glasshouses, across the island.

Many locals refer to them as vineries, which is how many of them started out. Vineries were built to grow grapes commercially as early as the early 1800s, although some wealthy islanders may have had small, private vineries before then. In fact, a small glasshouse located in the grounds of Candie Gardens is believed to date back to 1792, making it one of the oldest of its type in the British Isles. The very first vineries were designed as lean-to structures. This meant the frames and glass were built on the side of an existing building or sometimes a solid wall would be constructed to build against. Even later on, when larger standalone glasshouses were built, quite often a granite gable end would be included to add extra protection from the elements. The smaller, earlier vineries were occasionally installed with a Guernsey vine ladder. Thought to be exclusive to the Bailiwick, these almost horizontal ladders on rails allowed the growers to effectively pick fruit and prune their vines whilst lying down. There is a great example in the Victorian Walled Garden based at Saumarez Park.

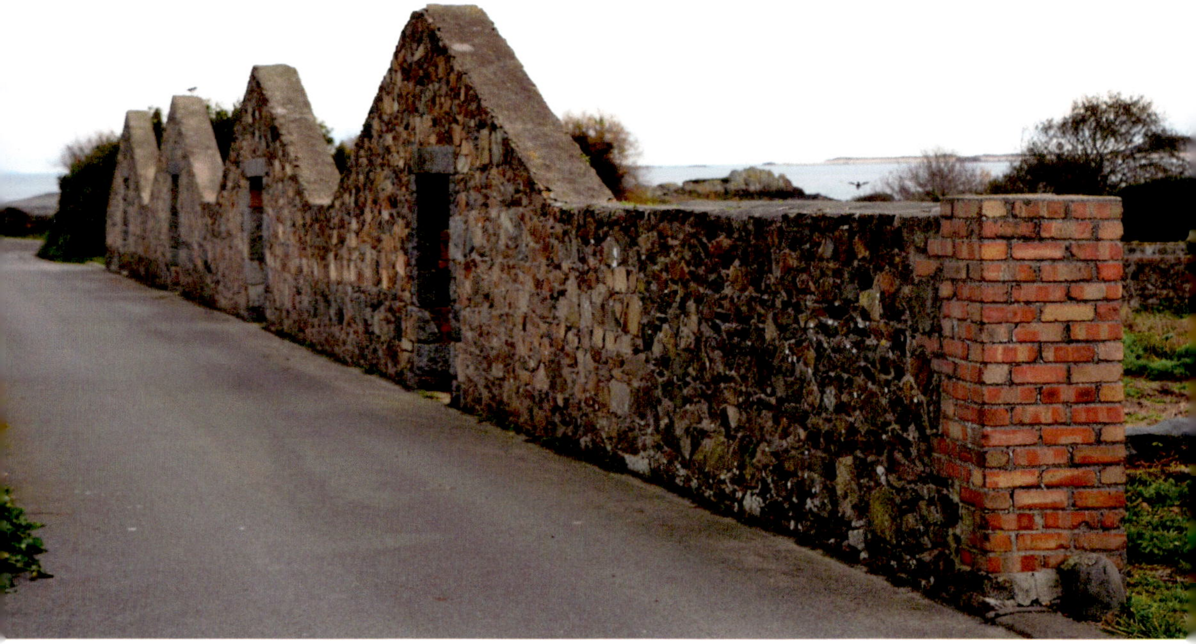

Above: End gables of former glasshouses. (Soo Wellfair)

Below: Guernsey tomatoes growing in a glasshouse. (Soo Wellfair)

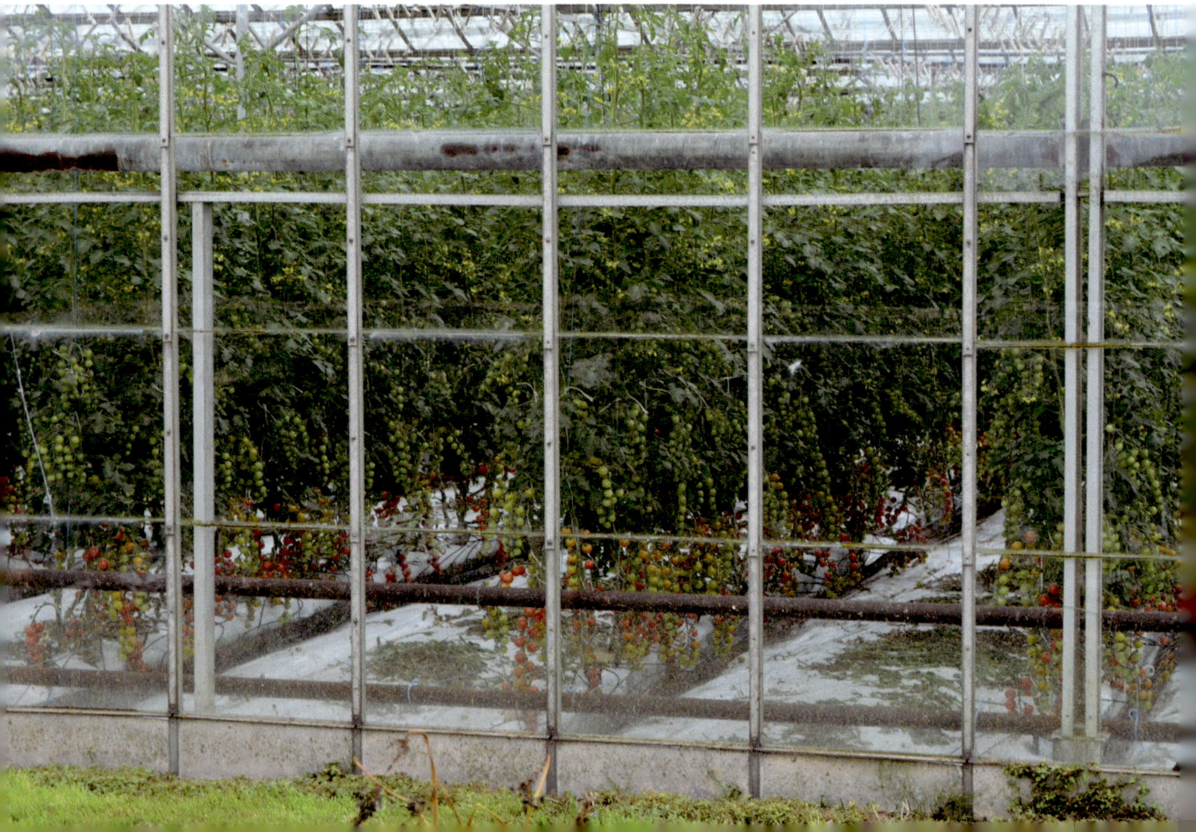

Grape growers started experimenting with growing tomatoes in the 1860s, making the most of the empty space below their grapes to cultivate this new fruit. More glasshouses were built specifically for tomatoes with many shipbuilders and carpenters switching to glasshouse building to meet demand. By the 1900s tomatoes had become the main crop in Guernsey and was probably the largest industry on the island at the time, until its decline in the 1970s. Between wars, around a quarter of the island's men were employed in the growing industry and by 1939 about 6 per cent of the land was taken up with glasshouses, with more still to be built.

Today it is quite a different story. Although some glasshouses are still used to grow produce, the majority of the remaining glasshouses are used to grow flowers. Growers have had great success in growing and selling cut flowers such as freesias, carnations and tulips and Guernsey clematis are famous around the world and regularly win awards at the Chelsea Flower Show. Whilst this has become a very successful industry in its own right, it is on a much smaller scale than tomatoes had been and unfortunately many disused glasshouses now lay dormant around the island.

50. Beach Kiosks

They may be simple in design, but the humble beach kiosk has become quite the icon of Guernsey's coastal areas. A familiar site, dotted mostly around Guernsey's coastline, the kiosks provide much welcome refreshments to beach users and walkers alike and no two kiosks are the same. There are larger kiosks made of

Pembroke Beach kiosk. (Soo Wellfair)

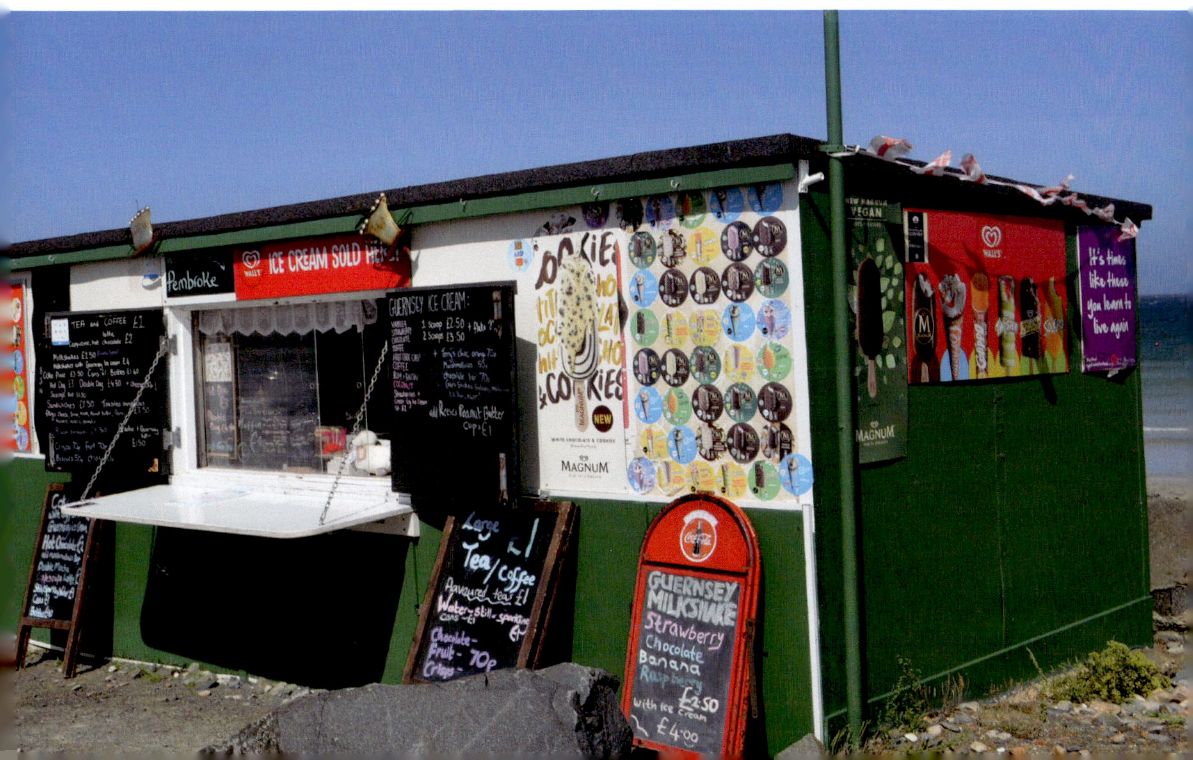

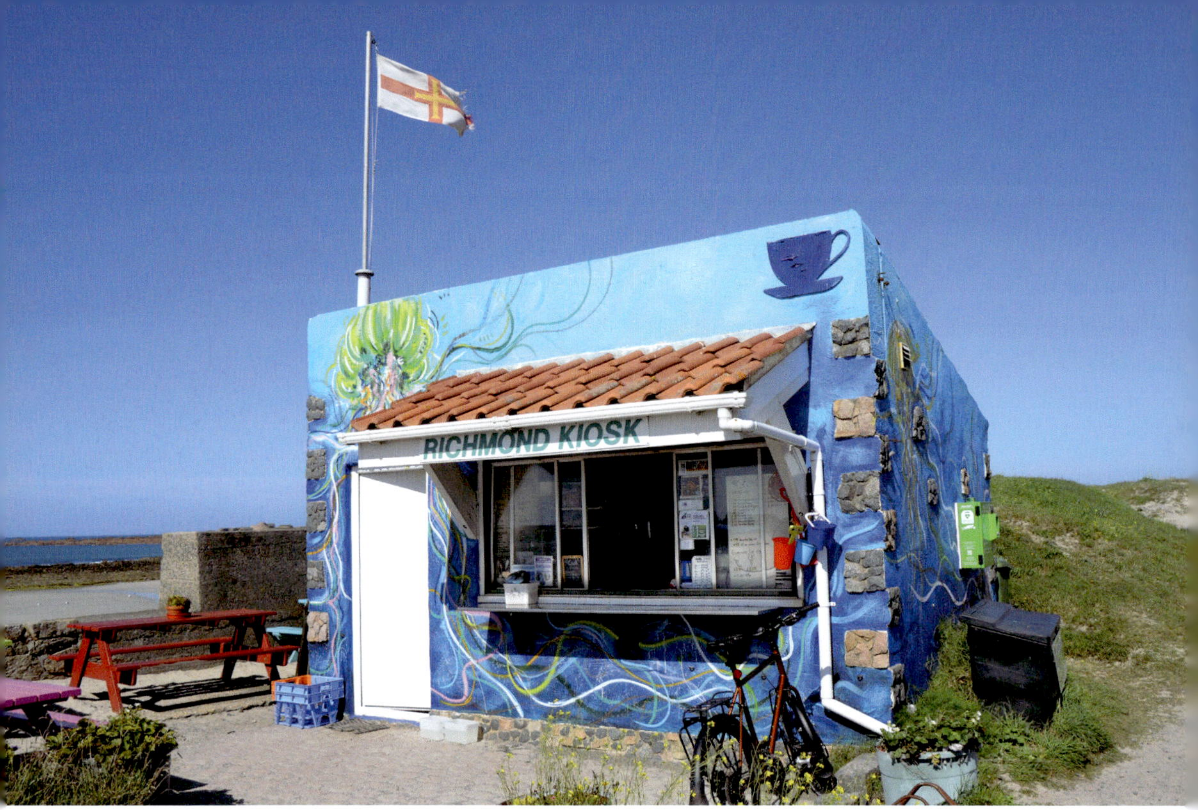

Richmond Beach kiosk. (Soo Wellfair)

Guernsey granite, smaller hut-like structures, some with tea gardens and some on wheels! It is believed that the kiosks were first constructed for the benefit of local fishermen coming back from sea, cold and in need of nourishment. The kiosks would provide a hot drink or a bowl of the local Bean Jar and fishermen would know the kiosk was open if the Guernsey flag was flying. This is still a tradition used with many kiosks today.

Bibliography

Printed Resources

A Tour of the Town Church of St Peter Port, pamphlet

Brett, C. E. B., *Buildings in the Town and Parish of St Peter Port* (Guernsey Press Co. Ltd, 1975)

Carman, J., *Guernsey's Trams* (2011)

Cogman, F., *The Story of St Martin's Church Guernsey* (British Publishing Company, 1966)

Collenette, V. G., *Elizabeth College 1563–1963* (Guernsey Press Co. Ltd, 1963)

Coombe, S., *John Wilson. Guernsey's Architect: A Celebration* (Blue Ormer Publishing, 2017)

Cooper, T., *Mansion, Manor and Merchant Houses* (Blue Ormer Publishing, 2018)

Croucher, A. E., *A Short History of St Stephen's Church* (Norprint Ltd, 1983)

Dafter, R., *The Guernsey Sentinel* (Matfield Books, 2003)

De Garis, M., *Dictiounnaire Anglais-Guernesiais* (Phillimore & Co., 1967)

Gavey, E., *A Guide to German Fortifications on Guernsey* (Festung Guernsey, 2023)

Grimsley, E. J., *The Historical Development of the Martello Tower in the Channel Islands* (Sarnian Publications, 1988)

Hares, Revd W. R. F., *A Pictorial Guide to the Parish Church: St Peter Port, Guernsey*

Jee, N., *The Story of St Marie du Castel* (Guernsey Press, 1962)

Ogier, D. M., *History of the Buildings of Guernsey's Royal Court* (Ozanne Publishing, 2004)

Priaulx, T. F., *Brief History of St Saviour's Church* (1964)

Salter, M., *Castle and Old Churches of the Channel Islands* (Folly Publications, 2001)

St Sampson's Church Guernsey, booklet

Online Resources

bbc.co.uk/guernsey
churchofengland.org.gg
governmenthouse.gg
guernseypress.com
megalithicguernsey.co.uk
nationaltrust.gg
priaulxlibrary.co.uk
societe.org.gg
trinityhouse.co.uk

About the Author

Soo Wellfair was born in Berkshire, England. She first visited and fell in love with Guernsey in the year 2000. She quickly adopted the island as her second home and now lives there with her husband and children, where she works as a gold accredited tour guide and freelance writer. As a tour guide, Soo specialises in walking tours which make the most of Guernsey's beautiful and varied terrain, and has a special interest in the folklore and social history of the island.